DAN CARTER

A TRIBUTE TO THE
ALL BLACKS' PERFECT 10

The only difference between you and Dan..... Sometimes Dan misses. :3

Happy 18th Mate!!

Dad x.

DAN CARTER

A TRIBUTE TO THE
ALL BLACKS' PERFECT 10

John Matheson/Celebrity Portraits

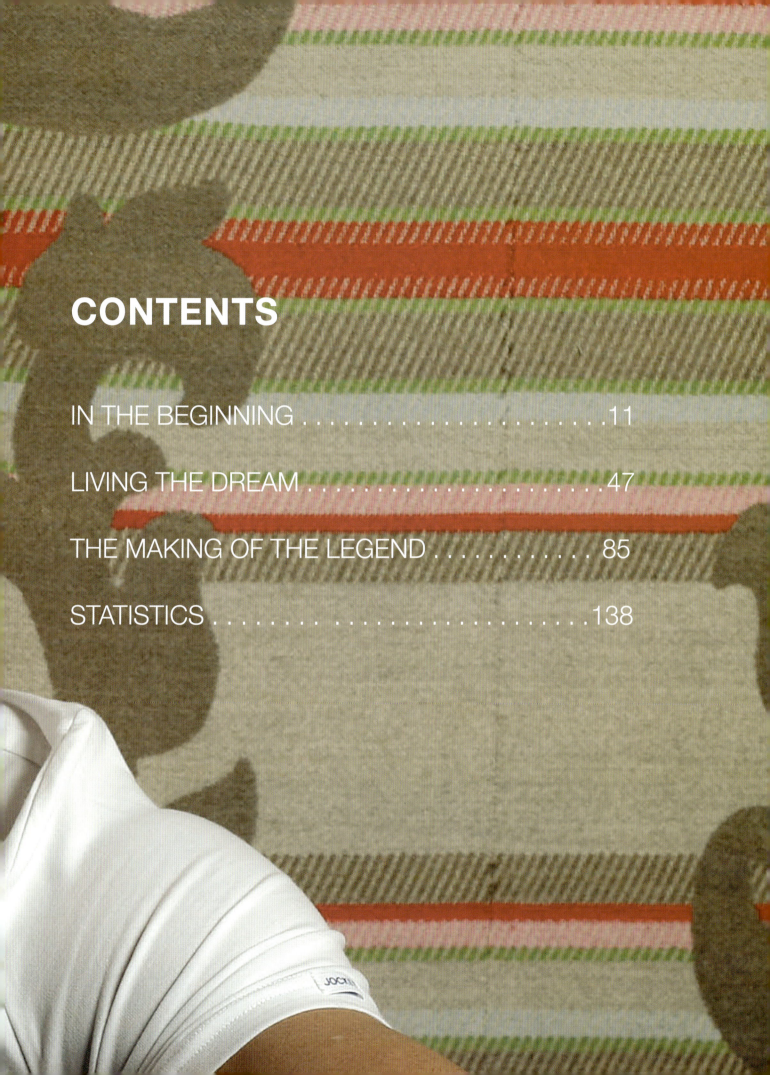

CONTENTS

Daniel Carter is all concentration as he lands a penalty against Wales at Millennium Stadium in 2006.

IN THE BEGINNING

THERE'S a school of thought in New Zealand rugby that keeps getting cut down to size. It happened when Grant Fox retired from test football in 1993 — the experts were convinced the rugby nation would never see another like him. But within two years in which we saw experiments named Marc Ellis, Simon Mannix and Graham Bachop, along came Andrew Mehrtens.

And while Mehrtens never dominated the All Blacks No. 10 jersey the way he should have — he lost possession of it to Carlos Spencer and Tony Brown at different times during his 10 years in the team — by the time he exited from the All Blacks stage the critics were at it again as they waxed lyrical about his time in black and forecast, once again, that New Zealand fans would never see another like 'Mercurial Mehrts'. The irony, though, was that even before Mehrtens played his last test in 2004, Daniel Carter had all but replaced him in the Crusaders team and was on his way to doing the same in the All Blacks.

Six years later Mehrtens — long since bypassed by Carter — has been reduced to an afterthought when it comes to the best No. 10 to have graced the globe's rugby fields. Wales's Barry John, England's Jonny Wilkinson, South Africa's Naas Botha, Australians Michael Lynagh and Stephen Larkham, and Fox are all in on the discussion. But any argument will be over if Carter adds 'World Cup winner' to his CV at the 2011 World Cup — such is his superiority over his rivals when it comes to the science of first-five-eighth play.

JOHN Kirwan was an early hero. And while five-year-old Daniel Carter didn't know it at the time, as he watched the giant All Black wing help the All Blacks win the 1987 World Cup it was being written by the authors of fate that one day, not far from his family's Leeston home, he would be offered a life lesson by the rugby great. A lesson which would help the humble Carter — struggling to come to terms with his new-found rugby fame and celebrity 'A' listing — deal with the reality of life as an All Black in God's Own.

The occasion was the opening of Carter's clothing store in Christchurch. Kirwan had travelled down from Auckland to film an interview for television's *Sports*

Café. It was the first time the two had met, Carter told the *New Zealand Herald*'s Wynne Gray in 2009. 'We did the job and he stayed around afterwards to chat, and we found we were on a similar wavelength. It was reassuring to discover that my hero on the field was equally special off the field. Too often people find out their idols are very different in real life, but JK was very down-to-earth, a very genuine, caring sort of bloke. He makes time for people and he was very helpful to me, talking about his experiences and discussing how to handle being in the limelight.

'JK was the marquee player of his era. He revolutionized wing play with his power and speed. His deeds were just magnetic at that first World Cup and beyond. I did not necessarily want to play on the wing, but I did want to play like him. He wanted the ball, he was always about scoring tries with his mix of strength, sidesteps, fends and pace. During his career JK also managed to indulge his love of surfing and has even managed to persuade me of the benefits. I started to learn and was looking forward to getting away to some spots like Biarritz a few times during my time in Europe, until I got injured.'

Biarritz, test football and fame were all in his future when Carter came to national prominence in 2003. He was a key player in the drama which would unfold during the Crusaders' Super 12 campaign — a campaign that brought an intense focus from the media on the relationship between coach Robbie Deans and star player Andrew Mehrtens. After some testing times in 2001 when Mehrtens had arrived for pre-season camp overweight and seemingly uninterested, the pair resolved any differences for the 2002 campaign when Mehrtens started 10 of the team's 13 games as the Crusaders cruised to Super 12 glory with a win against the Brumbies in the final at Christchurch.

But Carter would throw a spanner into the works for the 2003 campaign, which signalled the beginning of a World Cup year. Mehrtens had fronted for the pre-season trip to Australia highly motivated. Along

with fellow All Blacks Justin Marshall, Scott Robertson and Norm Maxwell, Mehrtens was in the last year of his contract. Of the quartet, only Mehrtens would be missing from the starting line-ups for the games against the Queensland Reds and NSW Waratahs. He found himself on the bench as Aaron Mauger was given his No. 10 jersey and Carter given Mauger's No. 12 from the previous season.

Critics watched with interest but the pro-Mehrtens brigade was silenced as Carter put in two impressive showings. Carter may not have been well-known outside the confines of Canterbury — he never made the national secondary schools team or the Under-19s — but within the province he had long been seen as *the* emerging talent. So there was no surprise from those in the know when he stepped up a level with ease.

Carter had a habit of taking chances when they came his way. When he was at Ellesmere High School — where he played initially as a halfback — a Canterbury secondary schools selector went to one of Carter's games to check out another potential talent who had been recommended to him. But it was Carter who caught his eye and, after his Sixth Form year, was persuaded to spend his last year in school at Christchurch Boys' High where he played at first-five-eighth, following in the footsteps of old boys Mehrtens and Mauger.

By 2001, his first year out of school, Carter was still out of the spotlight. He made only a few appearances in the High School Old Boys senior side, instead spending the majority of the year in the Under-21 Colts team. He wasn't deemed good enough to make the Canterbury Colts, and instead was selected for the province's Under-19 side. But he'd been noticed nevertheless, and, in 2002, was named in Bryce Woodward's New Zealand Colts side for the IRB's first Under-21 World Cup — a team which included All Blacks-in-the-making Ben Atiga, Jimmy Cowan, Luke McAlister, Joe Rokocoko, Anthony Tuitavake, Sam Tuitupou, Daniel Braid, Corey Flynn, Tom Harding,

Andrew Mehrtens was an early influence for
Daniel Carter at Canterbury and the Crusaders.

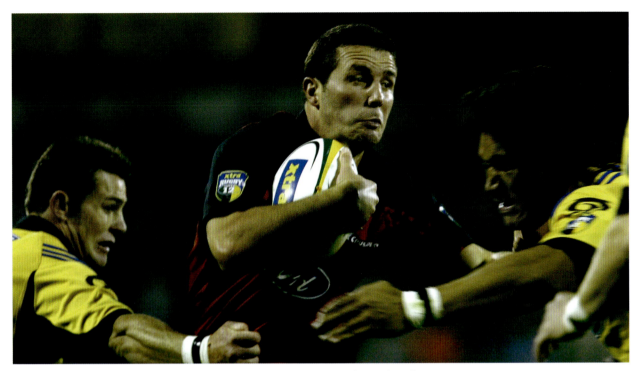

Aaron Mauger was the first to displace Andrew Mehrtens in the Crusaders line-up.

Sione Lauaki, Angus Macdonald, Brad Mika and Tony Woodcock.

McAlister had been selected as the first-choice first-five, but when he was injured the job was given to Carter, who played in all the games, including the heartbreaker against South Africa which saw the home team land a last-minute penalty in Johannesburg to sneak a 19–18 win and passage through to a final against Australia.

His form in the Republic — which included a 25-point haul against England — ensured he was drafted into Aussie McLean's Canterbury team for the 2002 NPC. The transition to senior rugby couldn't have gone better for Carter, as in his first three games — Ranfurly Shield defences against Marlborough, Mid Canterbury and East Coast — he scored six tries from second-five. With Mehrtens and Mauger back from the NPC, he would manage only three more starts for the team and make two appearances off the bench — the last coming in a semi-final loss to Auckland.

For Carter — who was doing a physical fitness trainer's course at Christchurch Polytechnic at the

time — it had been something of a perfect start to his senior rugby career. Canterbury's NPC squad had 19 All Blacks in it, and everywhere Carter looked he saw consummate professionals teaching him the art of rugby as well as schooling him in the culture of Canterbury rugby.

And by the beginning of 2003, Canterbury teachings had turned into Crusaders teachings. A first-up 19–17 pre-season loss against the Reds was followed by a 41–40 triumph against the Waratahs. And despite Mehrtens slotting home the late game-winning penalty, Deans opted to leave the All Black veteran out of the opening Super 12 game against the Hurricanes. It was a decision that left Carter embarrassed.

'I was a bit surprised, because I have always looked up to him,' Carter said. 'Just to get the chance to play outside him [in the 2002 NPC] was pretty exciting and both then and now Mehrts has been very supportive. But to be honest all I counted on getting in the Super 12, with Mehrts and Aaron Mauger in the five-eighths, was the odd run from the bench if I was lucky. Sometimes still when I look around the

Crusaders' dressing room and see the sort of players there I wonder "What am I doing here?" Still, it's good that all the hard work I'd done previously is paying off. But you can't sit back now that you've made it [to the Super 12]. You've got to pick up your intensity even more.'

For his part, Mauger didn't expect to see much of the No. 10 jersey. 'Dan's sort of in the position I have been in the last couple of years,' he said. 'I don't think you will see me in the No. 10 jersey too often while he's around. He's a very talented player and one who has a big future.'

The Crusaders opened their 2003 defence with a 37–21 win — Carter impressing everyone with a two-try effort. An injury to centre Nathan Mauger saw his brother move to centre, Carter to second-five and Mehrtens in from off the bench at first-five for the next game against the Reds. But Carter would again be the toast of the team after the 34–6 win with a stellar effort at first-five after Mehrtens limped off in the 28th minute.

Carter would retain the No. 10 position for the next six games before being swapped with Aaron Mauger and playing out the season at second-five. And after helping himself to a 21-point haul in the 39–16 semi-final win against the Hurricanes, the talk of an All Black call-up for the then 21-year-old hit a fever pitch. 'He has responded,' Deans said of Carter who had been 'hyped' by the scribes pre-game. 'He's a remarkable player and person. Despite what he has been able to do on the ground, he remains the same bloke, still working hard at his game, still seeking improvement. He remains unaffected by all the attention you lot give him. It's a good sign.'

With Deans doubling as John Mitchell's All Blacks assistant, it was also a good steer ahead of the naming of the first All Blacks squad of the year. And, sure enough, after the Super 12 final which saw the Blues beat the Crusaders 21–17, Daniel William Carter — who was still eligible for the New Zealand Under-21 side — had joined the biggest team around.

It was a great story, but not *the* story of the selection in that World Cup year. All Black veterans Christian Cullen, Taine Randell and Mehrtens were all left out of the squad which was selected for the year's first three tests against England, Wales and France in June. Carter had won his place because, unlike Mehrtens, he'd moved past the style of sitting back in the pocket and directing play from first-five. 'There are a couple of areas in Andrew's game we want him to improve on,' Mitchell said. 'We know a lot about his past form and what he can offer but the players who are ranked ahead of him [Spencer, Carter and Aaron Mauger] are a lot better taking the ball to the line and defending.'

Reuben Thorne, who had led the Crusaders through an unbeaten Super 12 in 2002, was named as skipper. And Carter was joined by fellow new caps, including his Crusaders teammate Brad Thorn, Hurricanes centre Ma'a Nonu and the Blues wing Joe Rokocoko and fullback Mils Muliaina.

Daniel Carter was first selected for the All Blacks in 2003. This is his first All Blacks squad — coached by John Mitchell and Robbie Deans.
Leon MacDonald (Canterbury), Mils Muliaina (Auckland), Doug Howlett (Auckland), Joe Rokocoko (Auckland), Caleb Ralph (Canterbury), Ma'a Nonu (Wellington), Tana Umaga (Wellington, vice-captain), *Daniel Carter (Canterbury)*, Aaron Mauger (Canterbury), Carlos Spencer (Auckland), Steve Devine (Auckland), Justin Marshall (Canterbury), Rodney So'oialo (Wellington), Richard McCaw (Canterbury), Marty Holah (Waikato), Reuben Thorne (Canterbury, captain), Jerry Collins (Wellington), Ali Williams (Auckland), Chris Jack (Canterbury), Brad Thorn (Canterbury), Greg Somerville (Canterbury), Kees Meeuws (Auckland), Keven Mealamu (Auckland), Anton Oliver (Otago), Carl Hoeft (Otago), Dave Hewett (Canterbury).

Of the new caps, only Rokocoko and Nonu were included in the All Blacks' run-on side to play England in Wellington — Carter, Muliaina and Thorn starting the game on the bench. For the beginning of a World Cup year there was somewhat of an experimental look about the side. Doug Howlett — one of the country's best wings — was at fullback; Nonu was at second-five because the selectors didn't want to disrupt his Hurricanes' partnership with Tana Umaga; and Carlos Spencer — the maverick Blues No. 10 who hadn't dominated a game for the All Blacks since 1997— was in the pivotal No. 10 jersey against the world's best, Jonny Wilkinson.

It was still a shock for fans of the Men in Black when Sir Clive Woodward's England recorded their first victory in New Zealand for 30 years with a superb defensive display at the Westpac Trust Stadium. Wilkinson spearheaded England's victory, kicking all the points in the narrow 15–13 triumph. But it was a superb defensive performance that laid the foundations for the historic win, most notably when the tourists were reduced to 13 men just after the break, with successive yellow cards for Neil Back and then Lawrence Dallaglio. England weathered a brutal onslaught from their hosts whilst they had the two-man advantage, and not only managed to shut them out but also to extend their lead, thanks to the boot of Wilkinson.

The win confirmed England's status as the world's form team and set a new England record of 12 successive test-match wins following previous efforts against Wales (50–10), Italy (45–9), Argentina (26–18), New Zealand (31–28), Australia (32–31), South Africa (53–3), France (25–17), Wales (26–9), Italy (40–5), Scotland (40–9) and Ireland (42–6). But perhaps most significantly of all, Martin Johnson's men struck

Jonny Wilkinson was key, as England upset the All Blacks in Wellington ahead of the 2003 World Cup.

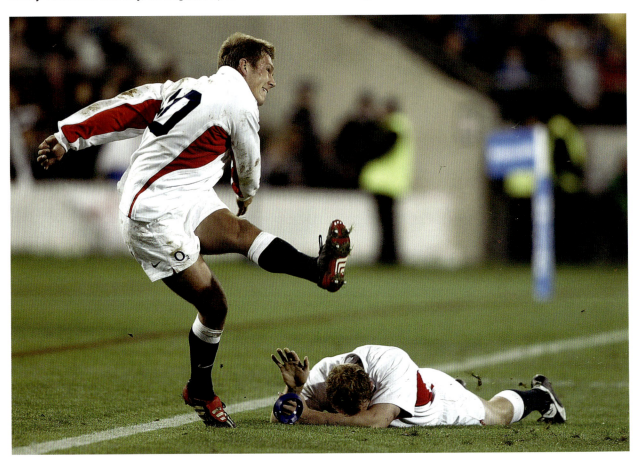

a huge psychological blow against their major World Cup rivals just four months before rugby's global extravaganza kicked off in Australia. However, Mitchell seemed unmoved: 'Psychologically it's fantastic for England,' the All Blacks coach admitted. 'But I don't think this loss at this stage is damaging for us. We will improve — there is no doubt about that. We showed signs of a lack of cohesion and we lacked composure at times. We have to learn, and we learnt the hard way tonight.'

Spencer, who had endured a nightmare time with the boot, missing four kicks at goal, was retained for the test against Wales, but this time he would have Carter alongside him. And Carter, having been in a losing All Blacks shed for the first time, knew the stakes were high. Failure against Wales was not conceivable. And Deans ensured both his young charge and the rugby nation as a whole was not fixated on the England loss. 'We didn't have a lot of time together [before the England test] and when we came under pressure the players responded in an individual fashion. It's something that comes with time. It's about trust in each other and combinations. It's the little things. If we are going to achieve anything this year, we have to do it as a team. We just have to improve. And we expect improvement.'

Mitchell and Deans got it against the Welsh as they carved up the Steve Hansen-coached Dragons 55–3 in Hamilton. Carter, who took on the goal-kicking responsibilities, slotted home six conversions and a penalty, as he, Rokocoko, Howlett, Spencer, Umaga, Meeuws and Mealamu all crashed over for tries. Carter's points haul saw him join an élite list of All Black sharpshooters to post 20 points or more in their test debuts. Carter's 20 points placed him sixth on the list of top all-time All Black scorers on debut.

Southland's Simon Culhane holds the record after a 45-point haul in the 145–17 drubbing of Japan at the 1995 World Cup. Spencer was second with 33 points in a 93–8 romp over Argentina in Wellington in 1997. Mehrtens was third with 28 points in a 73–7

caning of Canada in April 1995. Otago's Tony Brown supplied 26 points against Samoa at Albany in 1999, and Waikato's Matthew Cooper also notched 23 points when he won his first cap against Ireland in Dunedin in 1992.

Carter admitted he could not have dreamed of a better start to his All Black career. 'If someone told me I was going to score 20 points at the start of the day I would have been pretty happy with that.'

Carter did not have to wait too long before dotting down in the test arena. Carter crossed the Welsh line in the 46th minute after being put into space and palming off a tackle attempt from Wales wing Mark Jones. 'It was a pretty special moment, but it's just a bonus really,' he said. 'I was in the right spot at the right time.'

Carter had roomed with experienced teammate Doug Howlett on test eve, and said he was reasonably relaxed about his test debut. 'There's always pressure there when you're kicking goals, but it's something that I always enjoy doing so I take it as a challenge and really look forward to it. When Deansy said I was kicking I was really happy but I would have been supportive too if they'd said 'Los was kicking.'

Carter said a mild flurry of nerves dissolved once he landed his first kick to convert Howlett's try in the 20th minute. 'It was good to see the first one go between the uprights,' he said, while adding he 'dragged a couple to the right and that frustrated me a bit'. But Carter slotted some kicks from the sideline and finished with a seven out of 10 success rate — a commendable return for a test rookie.

Carter's skipper was quick to congratulate Carter after his try. 'It was a special moment for him,' Thorne said. 'It was his first test and to top it off with a try and to be taking the kicks. I thought he had an outstanding game.' And Mitchell, too, had been impressed. 'I can't speak highly enough of the youngster,' he offered, before Hansen, who'd watched the game from the opposition's coaching box, said Carter 'played like he'd been there all his life'.

Daniel Carter made his All Blacks debut in the test against Wales in Hamilton in 2003.

When the test side was named for the test against France the following week, Spencer was happy to see that his combination with Carter had been reinvested in. 'He was a lot of help; there's talk there,' Spencer said of the duo effort against Wales. 'And he brings in another kicking option as well if I need it. That's definitely a bonus.' Spencer had no worries about losing the goal-kicking duties to the new kid on the block. 'Losing the kicking didn't really worry me, I just look forward to getting out there and having a win. Dan did a great job last weekend and he'll probably do it again this week, so I wish him all the best.'

Not surprisingly the press attention on Carter increased ten-fold after his debut. And Deans was quick to remind his charge that a player's second test is often harder than the first. 'Obviously it's good for

DC to back up [against France],' Deans said. 'He's got a bit more accountability this week. Often the first test is the easy one . . .' Carter's new teammates had been a great help in keeping his feet on the ground. He was well aware of public expectations, but wanted to keep them from his thoughts. 'There's always pressure there, no matter what test you play. But after last weekend's performance, I'll have to concentrate on putting in another good performance. I've got a lot of respect for French rugby because they're very dangerous. They've got a strong forward pack and they've always had dangerous backs who love running with the ball. They've shown in the last year or two that their backs use good width and they can attack from anywhere.'

Carter was key in the 31–23 win against the under-

John Mitchell may have lost the World Cup, but he was responsible for introducing the likes of Daniel Carter and Mils Muliaina to the All Blacks fold.

strength French outfit, nailing four penalties and two conversions. The back-to-back wins put the All Blacks in a positive frame of mind heading into the Bledisloe Cup and Tri-Nations tests. The public, though, weren't convinced. The failure to select Mehrtens and Cullen — two of the country's most popular All Blacks in recent generations — turned some against Mitchell, while the loss to England led to more questions about Thorne's leadership.

The team's PR rating slipped even further immediately before the Tri-Nations when Anton Oliver

— the Otago hooker who had captained Mitchell's All Blacks before a knee injury in the 2002 Super 12 — was axed. He'd started in the tests against England and France, but struggled with his lineout throwing against Les Bleus and was eventually substituted. He joined Randell, Mehrtens and Cullen on Mitchell's scrapheap. Said Mitchell: 'We have a few things to work on still. It has been 16 years since we won a World Cup and in that time we haven't got things right. We've got a plan and we intend to stick with it.'

'TRUST me.' That was the message from John Mitchell as the All Blacks built towards the 2003 World Cup in Australia. His had been a divisive reign. At his first press conference following the naming of his first squad for the end-of-year tour to Ireland, Scotland and Argentina in 2001, he claimed he had dumped Christian Cullen because of poor form. It would be revealed the following day that Cullen — a living All Black legend — had pulled out of the tour before the team was named because of injury. There was also no room in Mitchell's squad for another All Black great, Jeff Wilson, and former skipper Taine Randell. Mitchell confirmed he'd rung neither of the duo before naming his team. The press conference set the tone for a strained relationship between Mitchell and the press pack.

And at the end of 2002 Mitchell incurred the wrath of many traditionalists when he rested more than 20 first-string All Blacks to give them a break ahead of the World Cup season. It meant that the likes of Cullen, Randell and Mehrtens — all of whom would be axed in 2003 — had one last chance to stake a claim in Mitchell's plans. Whether they ever had a chance to play a role in 2003 is debatable. Most people around the team, including senior players, are convinced the trio were nothing more than stop-gaps to fill the void left by the long list of absentees, which included Tony Brown, Jerry Collins, Ron Cribb, Greg Feek, Mark Hammett, Dave Hewitt, Chris Jack, Byron Kelleher, Leon MacDonald, Simon Maling, Justin Marshall, Aaron Mauger, Norm Maxwell, Richie McCaw, Anton Oliver, Caleb Ralph, Scott Robertson, Greg Somerville, Reuben Thorne and Tom Willis.

The tour was downgraded by many as being an All Blacks 'B' team, and at times they played like it. A 31–28 loss to England was followed by a 20–20 draw to the French and a 43–17 win against Wales. And with the first three tests of 2003 failing to see any real improvements despite the additions of the new caps as well as the return of the old guard, rumblings were commonplace as the All Blacks set out on their Tri-Nations journey in Pretoria.

Some good news was that Mauger was over his injury problems and was available for selection for the run-on side. He'd been on the bench for the tests against Wales and France but was unused. That changed in the Republic when he was selected at inside centre at the expense of Daniel Carter who dropped to the bench. The decision also meant that Carlos Spencer was once again the only recognized goal-kicker. 'Carlos will be doing the kicking and we have faith in his ability to do the job for us,' Mitchell said. 'He has been working hard at his place-kicking during the six-week camp and I do not believe we need to go onto the field with more kicking cover.' The other two changes to the side that played against France saw Keven Mealamu and Carl Hoeft take over from Oliver and Hewett at hooker and loosehead prop, respectively, in the front row.

It's fair to say that going into the test the jury was out, with many of the nation's press gallery unsure about whether the change would work. But any doubts were washed away with a sublime performance from the All Blacks, who served up a record defeat of the Boks with a 52–16 win. Doug Howlett and Joe Rokocoko scored two tries each, while Spencer, Mauger and Meeuws also scored five-pointers. And with Spencer converting four of the tries and slotting home three penalties, there was no need to introduce Carter to the action.

Not surprisingly, when the team fronted in Sydney seven days later for the first of the Bledisloe Cup tests there was no need for changes. Indeed, only one was made, at halfback where Steve Devine dropped out of the starting XV for Marshall. The Wallabies, stunned, were swept aside by a record 50–21 All Blacks triumph. Rokocoko made it 10 tries in five tests with a hat-trick, while there was also a try for Tana Umaga on his 50th appearance for New Zealand. Other tries from Howlett, Carter — who came on in the 53rd minute for Spencer — and Mauger ensured the All Blacks breached the half-century for the second weekend on the trot. England were no longer favourites for the World Cup . . .

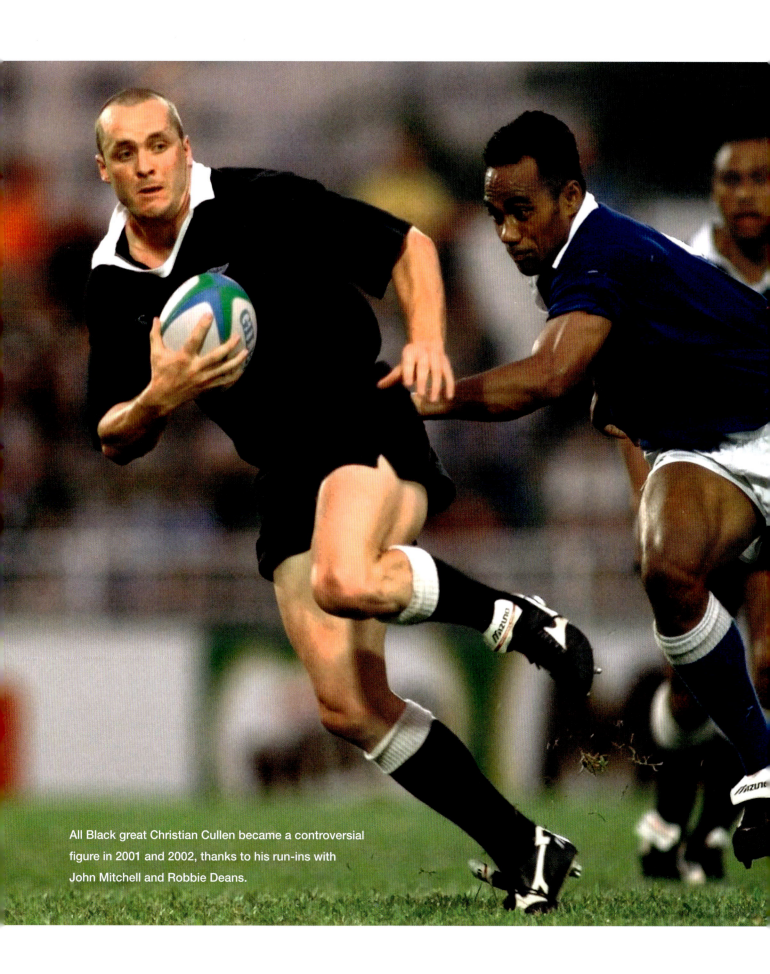

All Black great Christian Cullen became a controversial figure in 2001 and 2002, thanks to his run-ins with John Mitchell and Robbie Deans.

Tana Umaga would recover from an early fallout with John Mitchell to regain his All Blacks spot ahead of the 2003 World Cup.

Carter was enjoying his role off the bench. And even though he didn't play in the loss against England, he was beginning to understand the dynamic of the All Blacks dressing room. In 2006, *Sunday News* quoted Carter talking about his early experiences in the New Zealand shed: 'The All Blacks dressing room is not a fun place to be after a loss,' he said. 'You sit there in the dressing room, usually heads in hands, not daring to say anything for fear of breaking the heavy silence. Any conversations are brief and quiet. As a player you wonder what you could have done better, how you could have perhaps prevented the loss. If you made a mistake, you think about it, analyse it, not in self-recrimination, but in order to eliminate the possibility from the next game. The depression after a loss takes a while to lift. After a win it's much different. There's a lot of talk, and most of it animated; there's back-slapping and a general feeling of a job well done.'

After a 19–11 win against the Springboks in Dunedin, the Tri-Nations was wrapped up. A 21–17 win against the Wallabies followed, before attention

THE 2003 ALL BLACK WORLD CUP SQUAD
Ben Blair (Canterbury), Daniel Braid (Auckland), *Daniel Carter (Canterbury)*, Jerry Collins (Wellington), Steve Devine (Auckland), Corey Flynn (Canterbury), Mark Hammett (Canterbury), David Hewett (Canterbury), Carl Hoeft (Otago), Marty Holah (Waikato), Doug Howlett (Auckland) Chris Jack (Canterbury), Byron Kelleher (Otago), Leon MacDonald (Canterbury), Justin Marshall (Canterbury), Aaron Mauger (Canterbury), Richard McCaw (Canterbury), Keven Mealamu (Auckland), Kees Meeuws (Auckland), Mils Muliaina (Auckland), Ma'a Nonu (Wellington), Caleb Ralph (Canterbury), Joe Rokocoko (Auckland), Greg Somerville (Canterbury), Rodney So'oialo (Wellington), Carlos Spencer (Auckland), Brad Thorn (Canterbury), Reuben Thorne (Canterbury, captain), Tana Umaga (Wellington , vice-captain) and Ali Williams (Auckland).

There had been plenty to celebrate ahead of the All Blacks' challenge for the 2003 World Cup — the team pictured here after their Tri-Nations triumph at Eden Park.

turned towards Mitchell and Deans as they prepared to name their World Cup squad. It would, predictably, be contentious. Many had hoped that with the squad numbers swelling to 30 there would be room for some of the 'legends'. There wasn't. Cullen, Mehrtens, Randell, Oliver and Jonah Lomu were all missing. The omission of Mehrtens inevitably put the spotlight back on Spencer's goal-kicking. But with Ben Blair, Mauger and Carter in the squad, there was an abundance of alternatives should things begin to go wrong.

The All Blacks were placed in a pool with Italy, Canada, Tonga and Wales, and, if things went according to plan across all of the pools, were on a course to play the Springboks in a quarter-final, the Wallabies in a semi-final, and England or France in the Sydney final.

And they started the tournament the way they had hoped to finish it — with their strongest team possible selected and humming. With Mauger and Ali Williams injured, Carter and Thorn were called into the XV. It would be Carter's first test action since the win against Australia in Sydney — he was an unused reserve in the two home Tri-Nations tests. And there were no surprises as New Zealand romped its way to an 11-try 70–7 romp over Italy in Melbourne.

But there were problems. Umaga was injured in a collision with Spencer, and he would take no further part in the tournament. And Carter, too, was injured in the game — a knee injury the All Blacks kept secret until after the tournament. 'Unknown to everyone really is we had to manage Daniel Carter with a slight cruciate tear in the knee after the Italy match,' Mitchell told the current affairs TV show *Sunday* in his first major interview after the tournament. 'We had to [keep that secret] because Tana was down, Aaron was down and we just had to manage DC during the competition.'

The beginning of the end: Tana Umaga goes down with a knee injury in the All Blacks' World Cup opener.

Mitchell said he'd hoped Umaga would return at some point but it never happened. 'The card that didn't fall for us was Tana. It created an equation where we had the choice of Carlos [Spencer] or Daniel Carter or Leon MacDonald [to play at centre].' Mitchell went for MacDonald with his added goal-kicking abilities. It would mean a reshuffle of the backline which saw Muliaina taking over the No. 15 jersey.

In the Italian game, Spencer's goal-kicking radar was off (he missed three of his four attempts) and Carter, playing at second-five, would eventually take over the reins and slot home six conversions. He grabbed a try, too, along with Howlett (2), Spencer (2), Rokocoko (2), Thorn, Thorne, Marshall and MacDonald.

The inside-back combination was retained for the Canadian game. Ma'a Nonu was given the No. 13 jersey for the test, which featured nine personnel changes. Spencer's standing with the coaches was clear when he was awarded the vice-captaincy in Umaga's absence. 'We believe we are going to need all 30 players in this World Cup,' said Mitchell before the Canadian test. 'You can see with the example of Tana's injury. By giving all our squad a chance in this match, we are preparing everyone going forward. There is that opportunity to push for momentum but we believe we will gain more by involving our whole squad.'

Carter insisted the changes would have no effect on the All Blacks' attacking game plan. Carter had announced himself on rugby's biggest stage when he turned in a standout display against Italy, highlighted by a daring solo break from his own five-metre line.

Daniel Carter got on the score sheet in the 70–7 win against Italy in Melbourne.

Fed the ball by Rokocoko, he stepped inside and ghosted past four Azzurri defenders before setting up Doug Howlett for the score. It was a dashing 95-metre counter-attack from the All Blacks, and Carter said it was just an example of the mindset encouraged by the New Zealand management, no matter who is on the field. 'I think we have strengths all over the field and it's just a matter of giving the guys the opportunity and that's what we try and do,' said Carter. 'No matter where you are on the field, just have a look at the defence and if it's on, have a go. We look to open things up whenever we can and we are pretty dangerous at times. It's entirely up to you and if the opportunity is there you definitely take it. If it comes off, it's well worth it. It's definitely worth the go.'

Ten tries later, the All Blacks had a 68–6 victory over the Canadians. The standouts were Muliaina, who finished the night with four tries, and Carter, who landed nine of his 10 conversion attempts. Spencer impressed, too. Without the added responsibility of goal-kicking duties, he marshalled the team with aplomb.

With Williams — who had been recovering from a fractured foot suffered in the build-up to the World Cup — back in side for the game against Tonga, everything seemed to be falling into place for the All Blacks. Certainly the skipper felt as if the team was building nicely to its first real test against Wales once the Tongan game was out of the way. 'The build-up has suited us pretty well,' Reuben Thorne said.

Leon MacDonald was handed the goal-kicking responsibilities after Carlos Spencer lost form during the World Cup.

'It's given us time to try things training-wise. We've used that time wisely. Everybody needs game time. It's a difficult tournament and there will be injuries so everybody has to be prepared and ready to step in straight away. It's important to try everyone. There's plenty of time to work on the combinations and we're covering a lot in training anyway. The guys have got to know each other well. We're all switched on and enjoying each other's company.'

MacDonald was at centre as the All Blacks cruised to a 91–7 win at Suncorp Stadium in Brisbane — a position he would remain in for the rest of New Zealand's involvement in the tournament. And with Carter's knee tender, he also took on the goal-kicking responsibilities. And he had a match to remember, scoring once and landing all 12 conversion attempts for a personal tally of 31 points.

With Mauger back from his leg injury, he was

selected ahead of Carter for the final pool game against Wales — Carter's involvement in the tournament-proper all but over with only an appearance off the bench against the Boks still to come in the knockout phase. Deans saw Mauger as a supreme distributor. 'You've seen it in his performances to date this year, he's got a maturity about his game for a young man,' Deans said. 'He's a good communicator in the mix and he's got a very wide skill set. He's been a big part of our game. The fact that Aaron is starting this game is nothing against Daniel's performances. But in many ways it is timely. DC has carried a big load so it's good for him to get a bit of a window.'

The All Blacks cruised past a disappointing Boks side 29–9 in Melbourne's Telstra Dome, setting up the mouth-watering prospect of a semi-final against Australia on the same ground where they had blitzed them 50–21 in the Tri-Nations. The New Zealanders looked to be on the verge of a massive boost when Umaga — it would transpire later — was cleared by the team's medical staff to play. But Mitchell passed on selecting Umaga, telling the assembled press: 'It's been pretty close to five to six weeks since he's played any rugby. He's just not sharp enough. I couldn't put it any clearer than that. You have to be sharp at this level. That comes through speed and quickness and alertness.'

Ironically 'speed', 'quickness' and 'alertness' were all the domain of the Wallabies' performance in Sydney as they stunned the All Blacks with a 22–10 win. *Don't die wondering* was the call from one Australian newspaper on the morning of the semi-final and Eddie Jones's side seemed to duly take the headline onboard as a rally-cry.

Stephen Larkham looked to get a jump-start on the All Blacks with a drop goal attempt in the opening minutes, but his effort went wide with nerves playing their part. A break from Jerry Collins had Australia back-peddling soon after, and only a tackle from Wallaby wing Wendell Sailor on his opposite number Joe Rokocoko brought the move to an end. However, the All Blacks were soon pressing again from the lineout, and the ball went through the hands in the Wallabies' 22 to Mils Muliaina who looked to have dotted down in the corner under pressure from Lote Tuqiri. But the video official, Jonathan Kaplan, ruled that the ball had been knocked forward in the tackle.

The All Blacks looked determined to gain some reward for this spell of pressure, but when the centre Stirling Mortlock pounced on a loose pass from Spencer and raced 80 metres to dot down under the posts, the game suddenly had a whole new feel. MacDonald started to miss his kicks at goal — he

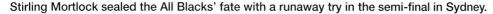

Stirling Mortlock sealed the All Blacks' fate with a runaway try in the semi-final in Sydney.

missed two penalties before a great take from Tuqiri spurred another surge from the Wallabies, and following successive turnovers Mortlock once again broke the gain line into the 22. The ball was recycled and, although the final pass was spun into touch, the All Blacks had drifted off-side and before the All Blacks nation could draw its collective breath, it was 13–0.

A Thorne try got the All Blacks on the board after halftime, but Elton Flatley's boot kept a decent margin between the teams as the All Blacks were condemned to play in the third- and fourth-place play-off instead of the final for the second World Cup in succession. After the French had been beaten in that game — the All Blacks winning 40–13 with Carter slotting home four conversions — Mitchell incredibly bemoaned the lack of experience in his squad; the very thing the selection of Cullen, Mehrtens, Randell and Oliver would have brought to the set-up. Said Mitchell: 'I believe we lacked maturity for [the semi-final]. Sadly as a group we had to go through that experience. We are young and maybe in some ways I underestimated that area.'

IT'S not what happens to you, it's how you respond. That was the message from Robbie Deans to his Crusaders-based All Blacks as they assembled to begin their preparations for the 2004 Super 12 campaign. Deans had been stung by the fallout from the World Cup loss. It was nothing he didn't expect. '[The ramifications of the loss and the experience of going through it] will always stay with me,' he said. 'I'll never be able to erase it totally. That's not a bad thing. I've got to use it.'

That was the same message he was giving his charges in Christchurch: 'To me, you always have the motivation to perform and deliver, whether through your own desire to achieve, or the standards you want to set and the group aspires to. It's not about the potential to fail. It's about the potential to succeed. There has clearly been pain and there are two ways you can respond to that. I think these guys, knowing

Robbie Deans didn't have time to dwell on the All Blacks' failures — there was a Super 12 to focus on.

'It's not what happens to you, it's how you respond.'

ROBBIE DEANS

the substance they have, will respond in a positive way. I've been really encouraged by the way they've come back together. There's real enthusiasm. That's a good indicator I hope.'

With Mehrtens re-signing with the franchise, attention from outside the province again focused on the relationship between Deans and the veteran first-five. The coach did his best to defuse any talk of friction between the pair, but admitted just how much game-time Mehrtens would get in the Super 12 was an unknown going into the season. 'Dan Carter and Aaron Mauger will factor into that decision,' Deans said. 'They are good players. Class players. I respect Andrew immensely and I, probably more than anyone, want and have put time into assisting him succeed. Last year he lost his ability to perform through his physical state, through injury and fitness.' It meant Mehrtens could not run as he used to, allowing other teams to hang off him and focus on players around him. 'They call your bluff if you're not prepared to carry the ball. But he's done a lot of work in the summer and is in great shape. As a result of that, his ability to perform is returning, his speed is coming back and with his experience he still offers a huge amount — he's a hugely capable player.'

Mehrtens's fitness was a bonus, as the Crusaders had lost six All Blacks from the previous year — Norm Maxwell, Scott Robertson, Mark Hammett, Mark Robinson, Greg Feek and Leon MacDonald had all moved on. Further bonuses were the growing influence of Richie McCaw on the side and the re-signing of halfback Justin Marshall. He'd been embarrassed in the semi-final loss to Australia when George Smith 'retired' him from the game with a hard, but fair, tackle. He had plenty to prove, and his motivation levels were at an all-time high.

As it was, the Crusaders made it all the way through to the final which was lost to the Brumbies in Canberra, 47–38. Carter's influence on the team had grown throughout the season. Standout moments included the game-winning penalty against the Reds

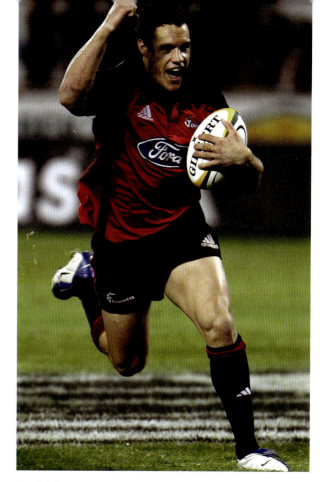

Daniel Carter would experience many highs in 2004, including this try against the Stormers in Christchurch.

in Brisbane, and 20-point hauls against the Brumbies, (twice) and the Cats in Johannesburg. He played in 12 of the team's 13 games. The only one he missed was when he was injured for the round-seven game against the Sharks in Durban. Ironically, Mehrtens was promoted to the starting line-up, after Carter was ruled out, but after the game was lost Mehrtens was banished to the reserves bench for the remainder of the campaign, and behind even the youngster Cameron McIntyre in the first-five pecking order.

All of Carter's outings for the Crusaders — which included six tries — had been in the No. 12 jersey. And that was exactly where the new All Blacks coaching panel of Graham Henry, Steve Hansen and Wayne Smith saw his future . . . for the time being at least.

Indeed, their determination to continue with Carter at second-five — outside Carlos Spencer and inside Tana Umaga — allowed them to bring Mehrtens back into the All Blacks fold, as the team prepared for the opening of their domestic test programme against

England, Argentina and the Pacific Islands. Another player called back from the international wilderness was Blues No. 8 Xavier Rush, who hadn't played for the All Blacks since 1998. Chiefs skipper Jono Gibbes, Highlanders fullback Nick Evans, Crusaders No. 8 Mose Tuiali'i and Blues second-five Sam Tuitupou were the newcomers.

The most noticeable omission was that of the former skipper Reuben Thorne — replaced by Tana Umaga as captain. 'I think Tana is a very positive role model for New Zealand rugby,' said Henry. 'He is highly respected by the players and is known in the game as a world-class player and has a huge amount of experience.'

It all made for an upbeat build-up to the arrival of England — the new World Cup champions — for a two-test series. Certainly John Mitchell was excited about the match-up, and was confident his former team would see off the under-strength Poms (who were without 14 of their triumphant World Cup squad). But he was disappointed that Spencer was set to continue as the All Blacks' first-five. 'Carlos is a wonderful talent but he has shown at the highest level a tendency to premeditate his attack and I don't think you could train that out of him,' said Mitchell. 'You've got to start building three years out from the next World Cup, so I'd start Daniel Carter.'

Carter was named at second-five in Henry's first test side. The main selection surprises came in the pack, where Gibbes, Keven Mealamu and Carl Hayman got the nod over Collins, Andrew Hore and Greg Somerville. In the new-look pack, Gibbes started on the blindside after playing most of the season in the second row, with Mealamu at hooker, Hayman at tighthead prop and Kees Meeuws at loosehead. Rush was preferred at No. 8, with Chris Jack and Keith Robinson in the second row and McCaw at openside. In contrast, the

The All Blacks pack would monster an under-strength England side in 2004.

backline was largely unchanged from the previous year, with Justin Marshall, Spencer, Carter and Umaga reunited along with the back three of Joe Rokocoko, Doug Howlett and Mils Muliaina.

Henry's era got off to a perfect start with straightforward 36–3 and 36–12 wins against Sir Clive Woodward's team in Dunedin and Auckland, respectively. It was a timely psychological statement ahead of the following year's British and Irish Lions tour to New Zealand, of which Woodward would again be at the helm. He'd certainly become aware of one DW Carter, who'd helped himself to 41 points over the two tests via a try, six penalties and seven conversions, despite the best intentions of Danny Grewcock who was banned after stomping him. To be fair, Woodward's team left all the wrong impressions in New Zealand, with the local media branding them nothing more than thugs.

Under the headline 'Dirty England a disgrace', the *Dominion Post*'s Australian-based columnist Spiro Zavos said the English team was 'nothing more than a rabble, a rugby equivalent of a lynch mob, intent on playing All Blacks off the ball and angering them into mistakes and indiscretions. A genuine world champion side, like the All Blacks in 1987 and the Wallabies in 1991 and 1999, set the standard in world rugby for the best practice. It does not try to set the standard for "allowable" foul play. Woodward's attempt to exonerate his players represents a disgrace to the leadership position he is supposed to now hold in world rugby as a knight for services to rugby. Services to thuggery is more like it.'

And the *New Zealand Herald*'s rugby writer Wynne Gray followed much the same theme, arguing England 'were shown up in both tests as a group who resorted to bully-boy tactics when their skills deserted them.

Daniel Carter evades the tackle of England's Joe Worsley during the All Blacks' win in Dunedin.

It has happened to all top rugby sides on the slide. When age hurts or skills deteriorate, the indiscipline escalates.'

The All Blacks, despite 10 changes, were too good for Argentina in Hamilton the following week and, with the top XV reselected for the one-off test against the Pacific Islands at Albany, cruised to a 41–26 victory — Carter chipping with a penalty and four conversions.

The build-up to the first Tri-Nations test of the year had been solid, but Henry knew that if he was going to have any chance of backing up 2003's title success, they'd have to be more accurate against the Springboks and Wallabies. Their cause wasn't helped when Richie McCaw was ruled out of the Tri-Nations with concussion. Marty Holah stepped into the breach on the openside, but, with Rush and Gibbes as the other loose forwards, it was difficult to see how the All Blacks planned to break the advantage line against Australia in the opening game in Wellington.

The difference between the teams in the end was Carter. He kicked three penalties to keep the Australians at bay as they clawed their way back into the encounter after Howlett had helped the score through to 13–0 with a try in the 62nd minute. The All Blacks won 16–7, and Umaga was convinced his second-five had a great future. 'The world's his oyster,' Umaga said. 'Hopefully I'll get to play outside him for as long as possible. I think he thrives on [pressure]. He loves that big-match atmosphere. If you ask him whether he can make a kick or not, he just laughs and says, "Of course I can." He's just got that confidence.'

Another who was impressed was former All Black captain and Sky Sport analyst Stu Wilson. 'He looks the part — which is always a good sign. Calm under pressure with a big-match temperament pretty well sums him up, and despite the challenges of more blockbusting players like Sam Tuitupou I reckon he'd be one of the first guys picked.' Wilson likened Carter to midfield greats like Irish legend Mike Gibson and French icon Joe Maso. 'They were players with similar

Daniel Carter gets away from England's Tom Voyce in the Eden Park triumph against Sir Clive Woodward's disappointing England side.

At the beginning of 2004, John Mitchell had been replaced at the All Blacks helm with Wayne Smith, Steve Hansen and Graham Henry.

attributes to Carter. Superbly balanced with great acceleration — the swerve, the sidestep, the kicking game — they had it all. Carter is just a boy but, hell, he could grow into one of the greats.'

With the Boks due in Christchurch seven days later, however, Henry knew his pack needed strengthening, and Gibbes was replaced by Jerry Collins. The other change came in the front row, where Greg Somerville returned to the starting line-up ahead of Carl Hayman.

Henry had another problem, too. A stomach bug had struck the team. Of the eight players affected, Carter was the most ill. The others were Marshall, Spencer, Muliaina, Rokocoko, Meeuws, Mealamu and Chris Jack. 'It's taken the edge off a number of our players, which is unfortunate,' All Blacks doctor Graham Paterson said. 'The good thing is it seems to

be something the boys can recover from fairly quickly. It is a bug that has got into the system and has spread from player to player.'

All the players would recover from the health scare in time for the test, but Henry had a scare of a rugby kind to deal with after their last-minute 23–21 win against the Boks. The South Africans, with only 23 per cent of the ball, scored three tries on the counter while producing such a ferocious defensive display that New Zealand were forced to rein in their attacking back play.

The Boks led 21–12 at halftime, and two second-half Carter penalties saw the lead cut to 21–18 with 11 minutes of the test remaining. Indeed, the All Blacks looked odds-on to lose to the South Africans in New Zealand for the first time since 1998, before Howlett scored a stunning try in the last minute of

play. 'Everybody would agree that was a game we could well have lost, but I'm proud of the commitment to go right to the end,' Henry said. 'Rome wasn't built in a day. We are trying to introduce new ideas and we haven't perfected them yet. I feel there are too many rugby teams who change for change's sake rather than perfect the areas they are working on. We are working on perfection.'

While nothing was said at the time, history proves that this game was a pivotal one for Carter. Not because of the five penalties he landed under pressure, but because backs coach Wayne Smith had seen limitations in Spencer's game at first-five. He was standing too shallow, and as a result was getting man and ball at the same time. His tactical kicking was at best average when he was under pressure. And as a result he was looking to move the ball to his outside backs instead of reacting to what was in front of him.

Smith was determined that Carter get a chance in the No. 10 jersey in one of the next two tests —

Highs and lows: Daniel Carter was in top form against the Boks in Christchurch, but injury struck in the loss against Australia in Sydney.

against Australia in Sydney or against the Boks in Johannesburg. But Henry opted to bring Mehrtens into the squad for the Wallabies game instead. Ironically, both Carter and Spencer wouldn't see out the action in the Bledisloe Cup game — Carter leaving the field with an ankle injury just after halftime, and Spencer being pulled from the action and replaced by Mehrtens in the 50th minute.

Carter had traded penalties with Matt Giteau for the teams to be level at 12–12 at halftime, before Spencer got in on the act and added one of his own with another from Giteau for a 15–15 scoreline. But a Lote Tuqiri try busted the game open, and not even Mehrtens could stop the rot as the Wallabies registered a 23–18 win.

Things would get worse for the All Blacks once they were in South Africa. Carter's injury kept him out of the test, and he was replaced by Sammy Tuitupou while Mehrtens got the nod to start at No.10 over Spencer who dropped out of the 22 completely. 'It's disappointing we've had to replace Carlos. But Carlos's form wasn't as good as we hoped,' Henry said. 'It's just a form thing really. He has been the number one fly-half for the last seven internationals but is just struggling for a bit of form at the moment. Andrew Mehrtens came on in Sydney and played pretty positively and we're just hoping he can continue that form.'

Mehrtens was delighted to be offered the chance to reclaim the prized No.10 shirt — the first time he'd worn it since 2002. 'I didn't expect to be in this position at the start of the year,' he said. 'It's a dream come true — I'm really excited. My face may not show it, and my voice probably doesn't, but I am! You probably don't know how much you cherish something until you no longer have it and obviously not being involved last year I had to take stock — and it's great being in the environment once again.'

Andrew Mehrtens had won an All Blacks recall after missing the 2003 World Cup, but couldn't help his team avoid defeat in Sydney.

This would be no fairy-tale return, though — the All Blacks suffering a 40–26 pounding. Neither Mehrtens nor Spencer would play for the All Blacks again. And as the Northern Hemisphere tour loomed, Henry, Smith and Hansen were making plans for the country's newest first-five-eighth.

It would be a move no one would ever look back at and question.

BILLY Stead did the job on the Invincibles' tour. The great Fred Allen captained the All Blacks against Australia in 1949 in the No. 10 jersey. Mac Herewini was Carlos Spencer before Carlos Spencer in the 1960s. Earle Kirton was the thinking man's first-five late in that decade and into the next. Doug Bruce won a Grand Slam. Wayne Smith and Grant Fox were the entertainer and the master-craftsman of the next generation, before Andrew Mehrtens and Spencer dominated the 1990s. Now, in 2004, it was time for the torch to be passed again.

The occasion of Daniel Carter's first test at first-five-eighth came in Rome. It was Graham Henry's first tour with the All Blacks, and the squad he'd selected reflected a move away from the scars of the 2003 World Cup in more ways than one. Steve Bates, Jimmy Cowan, Jerome Kaino, Casey Laulala, Luke McAlister, Conrad Smith, Saimone Taumoepeau and Piri Weepu were all named as first-time All Blacks, while Anton Oliver — unwanted by John Mitchell a year earlier — was back in the All Blacks fold.

'We're excited by the talent that has come through in the NPC and we are looking to utilize that potential to build depth in key areas that will position the All Blacks well for the challenges in 2005 and beyond,' Henry said. 'The tour is significant as it offers us a tremendous platform going into 2005 and what will be one of the biggest years ever in All Black rugby history with three extremely challenging series starting with the British and Irish Lions. We need to establish a solid base in terms of performance and selection options and the matches against Italy, Wales, France and the

Daniel Carter — seen here in the pre-game haka against Italy — was handed the No. 10 jersey on the 2004 end-of-year tour and hasn't looked back since.

Barbarians offer us every opportunity to do that.'

Carter got the nod to play at first-five ahead of Luke McAlister and Aaron Mauger and hasn't looked back since. Against the Italians he bagged 19 points, including seven conversions and a neat solo try following a kick ahead. 'I thought [Carter] was very impressive,' said Henry after the straightforward 59–10 win. 'With the exception of those two missed [conversions] I don't think he made a mistake. His general play was excellent. He broke well, passed well, kicked well. We're very satisfied.'

'Rotation' reared its ugly head for the first time during the Henry era the following weekend when he made nine changes to the starting team, including resting skipper and centre Tana Umaga to allow Richie McCaw to take the team's reins for the first time. 'There are no inconsistencies,' Henry argued when it was put to him that he was showing the Welsh little respect. 'I think we are fielding a very strong test team. We have got some strength in New Zealand in the centre, it is probably the strongest part of our game at the moment and we couldn't play them all. These are not wholesale changes; the nucleus of the side is there. We have done what we planned to do prior to leaving New Zealand and we are pleased we have been able to carry on with that programme — that is to have two strong sides play Italy and Wales.'

Mils Muliaina, Joe Rokocoko, Mose Tuiali'i, McCaw, Chris Jack and Carter were the only players to back up from Rome, and the tactic almost cost the All Blacks their first loss to Wales since 1953. Carter, though, held his nerve as he kicked three vital penalties and

'But look at Daniel Carter. He's going to be,
in my opinion, one of the leading All Blacks
in the next few years. The guy is an amazing talent,
and humble and relaxed with it.'

ANTON OLIVER

Byron Kelleher and Rodney So'oialo starred in one of the All Blacks' greatest performances: the 2004 win against France at the Stade de France.

converted Rokocoko's 54th-minute try to help seal a famous 26–25 victory. 'Everyone said if you don't bring away Andrew Mehrtens and Justin Marshall then we're asking for trouble,' Oliver said after Carter's heroics. 'But look at Daniel Carter. He's going to be, in my opinion, one of the leading All Blacks in the next few years. The guy is an amazing talent, and humble and relaxed with it.'

Henry reverted to his top line-up the following weekend in Paris, with Umaga, Byron Kelleher, Carl Hayman, Anton Oliver, Norm Maxwell, Jerry Collins and Conrad Smith all recalled, while Rodney So'oialo moved from blindside to number eight. 'There was a lot of competition for places at halfbacks, number eight,

prop, hooker,' said Henry. 'It was not an easy selection which is good. Picking the centres was probably the most difficult decision. One was obvious . . . the other was not but Conrad made a lot of progress mentally.'

The coach was rewarded with one of the great All Blacks performances — a truly stellar 45–6 victory courtesy of five tries. 'There have been some people who had been questioning the All Blacks and I think that was fair and [the players] just wanted to stand up and make a statement,' Henry said. 'It didn't happen this week, it's been happening for the last five months, trying to work towards producing something which is special.'

Four tries in 15 minutes either side of halftime to four

of the All Blacks' best — Collins, So'oialo, Kelleher and Carter — took the game beyond France. Ma'a Nonu scored the All Blacks' fifth try late, while Carter also booted 20 points. 'It felt great out there,' said Umaga. 'They put pressure on us but our boys stood up and we never wavered from what we were trying to achieve. Compared to the beginning of this year, I thought that was better . . . that collectiveness as a team, I felt was better.'

The All Blacks' performance had a big impact on the European media. Headlines in France's national sports daily paper *L'Equipe* such as '*La Marée Noire*' (The Black Tide) and '*La Punition Black*' (The Black Punishment) conveyed the general feeling towards one of the worst-ever French defeats. And England's *Observer* headlined its report 'Carter leads devastating dance of the All Blacks'. 'The All Blacks threw down a challenge to the rest of world rugby with an awesome display of power and pace that destroyed the European champions,' the story said. 'If the All Blacks are not the best team in the world at the moment, then someone, somewhere, is hiding a very good team.'

A STAR had been born in more ways than one.

Daniel Carter's rise through the ranks of New Zealand rugby was confirmed when he was named New Zealand's Player of the Year and Super 12 Player of the Year at the end-of-season awards. The All Blacks clearly had a genuine world-class first-five going into 2005 and the highly anticipated match-up with the British and Irish Lions. The potential of Daniel Carter v Jonny Wilkinson had the rugby world abuzz.

And off the field Carter was making waves, too. He was used to fronting up on the field, but he was left trying to sidestep a giant picture of his 'tackle' when he was signed on as Jockey's new underwear model at the end of 2004.

'I wasn't keen [on the idea] from the start,' *Sunday News* quoted him as saying. 'I am just a shy country boy and I don't seek publicity and parading my body

dressed just in undies didn't sound like a good idea to me. It just wasn't me. So it was a big "no" from me at the start.'

His girlfriend, Honor Dillon, and mum, Bev, weren't initially keen either. '[They] weren't all that keen and a few friends had a similar view. Their views gradually changed, though, as the ads developed and they saw what I knew — that everything was proper and above board.'

Carter was convinced to go ahead with the deal by his manager, Lou Thompson, and the shoot produced some of the most sought-after billboards in the country. Said Carter: 'I must admit to some embarrassment at seeing King Kong-sized photos of me in my undies. There was one big billboard in Durham Street in Christchurch and once, having seen it, I took great care not to drive past there again!

'Naturally I get a fair bit of stick from teammates and I expected that. But it was all good natured and they soon quietened down when I slipped them a few pairs of Jockeys. I was content with the way the whole thing worked and was gratified that the reaction wasn't critical.'

Macho rugby fans were hardly going to take pot-shots at Carter the way they had when Carlos Spencer famously stripped off for his Toffee Pops ads in the 1990s. Spencer was locked in a war for the No. 10 jersey with Andrew Mehrtens at the time — the country's support for the players was already divided so Spencer was an easy target.

In 2004 it was very much a case of Daniel Carter first and daylight second in the race for the coveted jersey. It was as though the would-be haters knew it was best not to upset the golden boy who held the key to the country's rugby hopes for the biggest year in New Zealand rugby history since the first World Cup was staged here in 1987.

In 2004 it was very much a case of

Daniel Carter first and daylight second

in the race for the coveted jersey.

LIVING THE DREAM . . .

THE year was all about beating the British and Irish Lions. It's true that the All Blacks' grasp on the Tri-Nations had been lost in 2004. And it's also true that at the end of year there was a Grand Slam to contemplate. In any other year, each could have easily been seen from within the team as the priority. But not so in 2005.

Four years after the historic tour, Daniel Carter revealed the goals the All Blacks had set themselves in 2005: (1) Beat the Lions; (2) Win the Grand Slam; (3) Triumph in the Tri-Nations. Said Carter: 'To a lot of people, a Grand Slam tour to the Northern Hemisphere is the one. It goes to show the way we play and how much it means to us. In the Southern Hemisphere, there is some really good, exciting rugby. I love being part of that. But in terms of the competitions there is not much history. Look at the Six Nations in Europe compared to the Super 14 and Tri-Nations. The fans love that tradition and it is a big difference there. The success rate of the Lions is not that great. But the amount of history behind them and the way their fans get in behind the team makes them special. The Southern Hemisphere teams play them so little, we're

lucky if we meet them once in our careers. It really goes without saying you want to make the most of those opportunities, that once-in-a-lifetime chance.'

WEEKS before Sir Clive Woodward arrived in New Zealand with his Lions squad, the greatest All Blacks of the modern generation held court with some key members of the media. Sean Fitzpatrick — a World Cup winner in 1987 and conqueror of the 1993 Lions — was predicting success for the All Blacks, and for Daniel Carter in particular.

'He is the full package,' Fitzpatrick said. 'He runs well in traffic, kicks exceptionally well, and does something a bit different to the other people on the team. He also gets the backs going, and having Tana Umaga outside him is a real boost because he's another key player and his leadership will be vital. It will be very interesting to see Carter come up against Jonny Wilkinson or Stephen Jones. They're actually all pretty similar. The way that Jonny is coming back is I'm sure very pleasing for everyone. People are saying that the All Blacks are going to target him, but it's going to take more than Jonny Wilkinson to beat

New Zealand. Carter versus Wilkinson should be a tremendous match-up.'

Not surprisingly Carter was buzzing as the first test in Christchurch loomed. 'It is going to be probably the biggest challenge the All Blacks have faced,' he said. 'We are coming up against an extremely strong side, and we will just go out there and try and play how we want to play, and if we do that well, then hopefully the results will take care of themselves. It is going to be tough.'

While the rugby world was anticipating the match-up made in heaven — Carter v Wilkinson — Woodward had other ideas. In the build-up to the opening test, the rumour that Wilkinson was going to be handed the No. 12 jersey instead began to circulate. Carter was unconcerned. 'I am not sure where Wilkinson will play. We will have to wait and see, but everyone knows what he can do in defence and attack — he's a strong guy who loves the confrontation. Our main focus is on us. Training is about what we want to do and what we want to get out of the game. We would have liked longer together, but the way it has worked out, we haven't had a chance with the Super 12 going along. But the time we've had together — three or four weeks now — we've covered a lot. I think we will have to step up another level from what we did against the French [at the end of 2004] if we are going to come out on top. You want to get the first one under the belt. Both sides see it as very important to come out with a win. Personally, I would just be happy with a win. I don't really care how we do it, just as long as we come out with the victory. We will try and get all the boys involved nice and early, so they can get their hands on the ball. It will be huge. They love their rugby in Christchurch, and I am really looking forward to it — I just can't wait.'

Rugby was on a high in the Garden City after the exploits of the Crusaders earlier in the year. The unity within the team was on show in the pre-season when All Blacks coach Graham Henry approached the franchise to see if it would allow either Andrew

Mehrtens or Carter to play for another New Zealand team to ensure both men would get ample playing time in before the arrival of the Lions. Neither, though, even entertained the idea — Mehrtens determined to end his time in New Zealand in a red-and-black jersey, and Carter desperate to win his first Super rugby title after consecutive finals losses in 2003 and 2004.

'Graham Henry informed us that of our group of players, he saw Daniel Carter and Andrew Mehrtens as being prospective first-five-eighth for the Lions series and as such he was keen for them to get as much exposure as possible,' Robbie Deans said. 'They were both protected in our 24 and it was our preference that they obviously be here with us. But they were given the opportunity to relocate and given a significant amount of encouragement, but they both declined that opportunity to stay with us.'

There was change at the franchise, though. Deans had made one of the toughest calls of his coaching career when he replaced skipper Reuben Thorne with Richie McCaw. 'Richie led through the NPC and the response [from the players] has been good,' Deans said. 'We are simply looking for him to carry on with that. But we fully expect Reuben Thorne to continue to lead by example. We try and develop leadership, and these guys are not only good teammates in the way they work for each other, but they are also very good mates. [The decision] won't affect Reuben's mana within the group. In fact, I'd suggest it will probably grow. It doesn't take away from Reuben in terms of what he's achieved. The opportunity now rests with Richie to carry it on.'

It didn't take long for the masterstroke of retaining Mehrtens and Carter to pay off. In the first round of the competition — with Scott Hamilton injured and Leon MacDonald on his way back from a stint in Japan — there was an opening at fullback. The job was given to Carter, and Mehrtens was back in the No. 10 jersey — his first start for the franchise since his horror show in Durban a year earlier.

Unfortunately for Mehrtens, his comeback game

Jonny Wilkinson was back in New Zealand, this time with the Lions — and the rugby world couldn't wait for his clash with Daniel Carter.

would also end in defeat — the defending champion, Brumbies, proving too good in Canberra winning 32–21. Carter was restored to his rightful position for the next game against the Chiefs and made his point — in case it had to be made — with a try, a penalty and six conversions in a 50–18 win.

Carter played eight of the next 11 games in the No. 10 jersey — the exceptions being the round-robin games against the Cats and Hurricanes when he was rested and the game in Sydney against the Waratahs when he donned the No. 12 jersey in a tactical move which saw Mehrtens score a vital try in the 33–27 win.

That victory was one of nine out of 11 as the Crusaders stormed into the semi-finals and a date with the star-studded Hurricanes. All Blacks captain Tana Umaga was at the top of his game, and the Canes were favoured by many to get out of Christchurch with a victory, with the likes of Jerry Collins, Rodney So'oialo and Ma'a Nonu all playing the best rugby of their careers.

But there were frailties in Colin Cooper's side, too — that much was clear when they lost home games to the Bulls and Highlanders in the round robin. And their halfback, first-five, second-five combination of Piri Weepu, Jimmy Gopperth and Tane Tuipulotu were hopelessly exposed in the semi, as was Chris Masoe in his personal match-up with McCaw. 'What can you say . . . ' Umaga gasped after the Crusaders' 47–7 romp. 'That was just a brilliant effort from the Crusaders, something we've come to expect from them.'

Predictably the line-up for the final against the Waratahs was unchanged from the side that had defeated the Canes: Leon MacDonald, Rico Gear, Caleb Ralph, Aaron Mauger, Scott Hamilton, Daniel Carter, Justin Marshall, Mose Tuiali'i, Richie McCaw (captain), Reuben Thorne, Ross Filipo, Chris Jack,

The Crusaders kept up their domination of Super rugby ahead of the test season, with victory in the final against the Waratahs.

Greg Somerville, Corey Flynn, Dave Hewett. Reserves: Tone Kopelani, Campbell Johnstone, Sam Broomhall, Johnny Leo'o, Jamie Nutbrown, Andrew Mehrtens, Casey Laulala. And predictably, too, the Crusaders won the Christchurch final 35–25 — cementing their status as the most dominant team of the Super 12 era.

The home side took a 14–6 halftime lead, scoring the only try of the first half, through Scott Hamilton in the 13th minute after an explosive break and kick through by winger Rico Gear. Two tries in the opening 23 minutes of the second half broke the back of the visitors, before centre Caleb Ralph's 67th minute effort gave the Crusaders a 35–6 lead. It had been the perfect farewell for Marshall, Hewett, Maxwell and Mehrtens, who were all headed offshore. And the rugby the team had served up had been near-perfect as well — none more impressed than the All Blacks coach who was readying himself to name the squad for the series against the Lions. 'I thought their display in the semi-final was one of the best displays I've seen at Super 12 level since 1996, the start of the professional period,' Henry said.

However, just seven Crusaders made the first squad of the domestic test programme for the season-opening hit-out against Fiji at Albany — the All Blacks' only test before the Lions trilogy. Five players were named for the first time — Chiefs' Sosene Anesi (fullback) and Sitiveni Sivivatu (wing), Highlanders lock James Ryan, Blues hooker Derren Witcombe, and Johnstone — the Crusaders prop.

Witcombe, Ryan and Sivivatu were given run-on debuts against the Fijians in a 91–0 romp, while Anesi and Johnstone joined the party from the bench. Sivivatu — the Fijian-born winger who only qualified for New Zealand months before the game — became the first All Black to score four tries on his test debut, as he dazzled the crowd with electric footwork and clever handling. Umaga and Doug Howlett scored two apiece, and the All Blacks also worked tries for Carter, Somerville, Mauger, So'oialo, Ali Williams, Keven Mealamu and Mils Muliaina.

There was, of course, little to take from the game other than the solidification of the partnership between Carter and Aaron Mauger — only their second game together for the All Blacks at No. 10 and No. 12, respectively. It was clearly the preferred combo going into the Tri-Nations, with Umaga restored to centre after he'd played at second-five in his two test appearances in Europe in 2004. It was a move that Umaga embraced. 'Aaron's a great distributor, good communicator. He's got all the skills of a first-five but one place out,' Umaga said. 'And he's a good defender. He's what you want in a player, he's got it all. With DC [Carter] there with his left foot, they balance each other well.'

The try-fest had many believing in the likes of former All Blacks coach Laurie Mains and All Blacks greats Andy Haden and Zinzan Brooke who had all predicted a 3–0 series scoreline against the Lions. But the skipper was keen for the rugby nation not to expect too much too soon. The 45–6 defeat of France in Paris in their last test of 2004 was the standard many were expecting to hit when the players took to the field for the opening bout against the Lions.

'We were a new bunch of guys on that tour and what did it take us, three games?' Umaga said.

'Who's to say [this time] it could be sooner, it could be longer. It's only been a couple of days and we've had to fit in a lot of content in that time but it's coming together slowly. For most of us it's a reminder of the stuff we went over on the end-of-year tour. It's about getting the guys who weren't there up to speed. We can't rest on a couple of guys being brilliant — the likes of Dan Carter and Richie McCaw, doing it by themselves. We've got to all do our jobs.'

Umaga had an ally in the form of Fitzpatrick. The 128-game All Blacks veteran was expecting the All Blacks to edge the series 2–1. However, he believed the Lions had a tremendous chance to gain the upper hand in the opening fixture between the two sides. 'I think the Lions have a real opportunity to win the first Test, and they need to win that first one if they are

All Black wing Sitiveni Sivivatu was evidence of the overpowering artillery the All Blacks coaching staff had at their disposal.

to have any chance of winning the series,' Fitzpatrick added. 'I think their preparation will be excellent in terms of playing Argentina, but it will be a real eye-opener for some of the guys who haven't toured, because it's rugby 24/7 in New Zealand.

'In contrast the All Blacks only play Fiji, so their build-up isn't great. I think they will probably win that first test and then the All Blacks will win the next two, purely because it's in New Zealand. I'm a huge believer that we can beat them out wide, and we've got to take them on in the forwards. My only concern is the intensity of the Super 12 compared to the Premiership [in England] but I think we'll be able to get up to speed quick enough. People are talking about the number of players they are taking, but the more the better for us in terms of seeing the Jonny Wilkinsons, and the Lawrence Dallaglios and the Brian O'Driscolls. It will be a phenomenal tour.'

Those numbers swelled to 46 when Welsh loose forward Ryan Jones was added to the squad to cover for the injured Simon Taylor. 'How many is that now?' Henry cheekily asked the press when told of Jones's inclusion. 'If we name more than 22 I get criticized by old All Blacks for cheapening the shirt. . .' The war of words was on, and preceded the naming of the All Blacks squad for the first test. Anton Oliver was brought in, while notable omissions included Waikato forwards Jono Gibbes and Marty Holah who had both been outstanding in New Zealand Maori's 19–13 defeat of the Lions. Rokocoko, who had scored 27 tries in 23 tests, missed out with Howlett, Sivivatu and Rico Gear covering wing. Another inclusion was MacDonald — back in the international fold after spending the 2004 season in Japan.

THE ALL BLACKS SQUAD WHICH TOOK ON, AND BEAT, THE 2005 BRITISH AND IRISH LIONS
Backs: Mils Muliaina (Auckland), Leon MacDonald (Canterbury), Doug Howlett (Auckland), Rico Gear (Nelson Bays), Sitiveni Sivivatu (Waikato), Ma'a Nonu (Wellington), Conrad Smith (Wellington), Tana Umaga (Wellington, captain), Aaron Mauger (Canterbury), *Daniel Carter (Canterbury)*, Byron Kelleher (Waikato), Justin Marshall (Canterbury).
Forwards: Rodney So'oialo (Wellington), Mose Tuiali'i (Canterbury), Richie McCaw (Canterbury, vice-captain), Jerry Collins (Wellington), Sione Lauaki (Waikato), Chris Jack (Canterbury), Ali Williams (Auckland), James Ryan (Otago), Carl Hayman (Otago), Campbell Johnstone (Canterbury), Greg Somerville (Canterbury), Tony Woodcock (Auckland), Keven Mealamu (Auckland), Anton Oliver (Otago).
*Trained with squad: Derren Witcombe (Auckland) and Jono Gibbes (Waikato).

As the first test approached, the rumour that Woodward would keep Wilkinson away from a one-on-one confrontation surfaced again. When quizzed about where England's 2003 World Cup hero should play, Carter said that, even though he rated him first as a No 10, he'd be wary of 'Wilko' wherever he played. 'He's probably equally good in both positions although personally I see him more in the first-five role,' Carter told the UK press. 'Everyone knows what he can do on defence, and on attack he's a strong man and loves the confrontation.' Interestingly, even though they were both left-footers and quality goal-kickers, Wilkinson, said Carter, had cast little influence over his own career.

'We both play the same position and are left-footers but I think we've got pretty different games. Obviously he's a great player and he works hard on his game. That's probably the comparison, I love getting out there and doing the work, keeping my skill base high.'

For his part, Wilkinson was happy to play anywhere for the Lions — he just wanted to be a part of this rugby story. 'As long as I'm in a position where I can use my skills and add to the team,' Wilkinson said. 'One thing I wish I could do more is be more of an open field player, take the numbers off the back sort of thing. Brian O'Driscoll and Jason Robinson are great examples of people who can suddenly pop up anywhere and play as they want to play. New Zealand

have shown with the likes of Aaron Mauger, Dan Carter and, in the past, Lee Stensness that have been great decision-making ball players playing in and out of that position. They've shown it can be done.'

Woodward decided to parade eight of his England World Cup-winning squad in his first test team, with Wilkinson in at second-five outside Wales's No. 10 Stephen Jones. And, in another surprise move, fullback Josh Lewsey lined up on the right wing, with his England colleague Jason Robinson at fullback. Lewsey, Robinson and Wilkinson were joined in the starting XV by fellow World Cup winners Julian White, Ben Kay, Richard Hill, Neil Back and Martin Corry, while there were four more on the bench — Steve Thompson, Danny Grewcock, Matt Dawson and Will Greenwood.

The 'Dad's Army' vibe of the Lions was in stark

Brian O'Driscoll (third from the right) looks on during the All Blacks haka ahead of the first test in Christchurch. Within minutes, his tour would be over.

contrast to the side named by Graham Henry.

There were five changes from the side that beat Fiji; Hayman and MacDonald joined the team, while Mealamu, Jack and Marshall assumed starting spots after manning the bench in Albany. There was excitement-plus in the backline — something on paper that at least the Lions wouldn't be able to match. Marshall would be servicing Carter, Sivivatu, Mauger, Umaga, Howlett and MacDonald — with Kelleher, Muliaina and Gear awaiting their chance from the bench.

Carter admitted that preparation for the series had been far from perfect, saying the romp against Fiji hadn't been ideal. 'It would have been good to have a tighter sort of test before the Lions,' he said. 'We'd like longer together but that's the way it's worked out. I was probably expecting a bit more from the Fijians . . . it's going to be totally different this weekend. 'It's going to be the biggest challenge the All Blacks have probably ever faced. [Paris] was a good step for us back then. We've got some new players in the side now but a lot of the same guys are still there. We've just looked to continue on that sort of form. We've got a new challenge with the Lions; they're going to be quite a lot stronger than the French side that we faced. I think we'll have to step up another level from what we did against France if we're going to come out [ahead].'

Carter needn't have worried. The gulf between the two teams was massive — the All Blacks, with tries to Ali Williams and Sivivatu and 10 points from Carter's boot — cruised to a 21–3 victory. Their tactic of exposing Robinson at fullback worked wonderfully. Mauger and Umaga controlled the midfield battle, while Williams dominated the lineouts, and McCaw made Back look like an old man. To add insult to injury, Hayman, Mealamu and Tony Woodcock completely dominated the battle of the front rows — an area where the Lions had expected to dominate.

Messieurs Mains, Haden and Brooke looked like geniuses post-game, but the All Blacks' performance

never received the plaudits it deserved because of the injury sustained by O'Driscoll in the first minutes of the game. The contentious moment would be replayed on the television, by different coaching panels and in the court of public opinion in the seven days between the two tests. O'Driscoll claimed a spear tackle had ended his tour, while Umaga and Mealamu — the two players involved in the tackle — insisted nothing sinister had gone on. The Lions management then made the fatal mistake of questioning Umaga's character. The All Blacks rallied around their skipper and took out their frustration on Woodward's men in Wellington — a test that will forever be remembered as Carter's coming of age.

Carter scored two tries, kicked five penalties, and slotted four conversions as the All Blacks clinched the series with a 48–18 victory. He dominated the test as he produced the complete performance to outshine Wilkinson who had been restored to his rightful No. 10 jersey. 'He had an exceptional game. He kicked every goal, he broke the line, he scored a number of tries, his defence was superb. He navigated the ship, for a 23-year-old, quite outstandingly,' said Henry. 'He did have an outstanding game. I thought he was very special.'

British rugby writers lauded the gulf in class between the Carter-inspired All Blacks and the tactically deficient Lions. In *The Independent*, Chris Hewett said Carter had claimed the title of world's best first-five-eighth from Wilkinson, who departed with a shoulder injury late in the match. He labelled it 'the passing of a mantle, and possibly of an era'. 'Wilkinson, the man who dropped the goal that won a World Cup for England, had been considered the best outside-half on the planet for the best part of five years,' Hewett wrote. 'Yes, injuries had cramped his style, but even

Daniel Carter was at his sublime best in the second test in Wellington, as the All Blacks claimed the Lions series 2–0 with a 48–18 victory.

during the weeks and months when Wilkinson was completely down on his luck, there had still been a lingering suspicion in many minds that his work in the No. 10 shirt was more effective than anyone else's. We can safely forget all about that now, for Carter is the new prince of the position.'

Former England lock Paul Ackford joined in the Carter superlatives in the *Telegraph*, labelling his contribution 'sublime' and hailing him 'the new superstar of the global game, beyond any question'.

'In some ways this was worse than the Christchurch fiasco,' Ackford wrote. 'There, the Lions had the excuse of a dysfunctional lineout to fall back on. Last night it was across all areas of the game where the gulf in class was evident. The All Blacks to a man were better than the Lions, but in Daniel Carter we saw one of the finest international displays at outside-half, even if he did have the ball on tap, with Byron Kelleher outstanding inside him.'

Henry was also quick to praise his captain, who

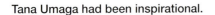
Tana Umaga had been inspirational.

produced one of his finest performances in the black jersey after his difficult week. Umaga scored the All Blacks' first try and had a hand in three of the other four, as his ability to offload in the tackle and his powerful running on attack created space for his fellow backs. 'I thought [Umaga] was quite fabulous,' said Henry. 'He just showed the character he has got to play an outstanding game as captain and as a player.'

Another who was impressed was Luke McAlister. With Carter nursing an injured shoulder, the North Harbour player was handed the All Blacks No. 10 jersey for the third test in Auckland. He admitted following Carter's 33-point haul was daunting. 'First-five's a huge position in the team, it's the driver of the car, I suppose,' he said. 'To fill Dan Carter's boots will be tough but hopefully I can do that.' Asked about Carter's performance in Wellington, McAlister was to the point: 'I just thought Dan was the man. He was God, wasn't he? He's injured and I'm sure he'll be back soon. This gives me the opportunity now and hopefully I can come in and take it.'

The All Blacks' catch-cry as they chased a 3–0 whitewash was one of doing it for the players who were missing. As well as Carter, McCaw, MacDonald, Mauger and Hayman were also missing from the Eden Park line-up. 'This is exactly what we need,' Henry said. 'It gives us another challenge, four or five changes from last week, one in the role of No. 10, who really navigates the team. It's now how the team pulls together to make it the best it can be. It's a challenge for us, and I'd like to see how we handle it. I've got every confidence they'll handle it well.'

He was right. McAlister kicked six from six as he collected 13 points in the 38–19 win. Umaga was again a star — scoring two tries along with solitary efforts from Williams, Gear and Conrad Smith — as the All Blacks again had too much pace and finishing power for the hapless tourists.

Lions back Josh Lewsey hailed New Zealand as rugby's new world leaders after the Lions had become the first to draw a blank Down Under since

1983, and after they'd conceded a record 107 points, scoring just three tries, while conceding 12. 'We were pretty ashamed of our first-test performance, and in the second test we gave it everything but just weren't good enough and got beaten by a better side,' he said. 'We tried to take the lessons onboard, and we tried to play with ball in hand a bit more, but it takes time to develop. Natural ability will only get you so far, and you have to put your hand up and say they were better than us. They are leading the way in terms of the way the game is played at the moment, but you cannot blame anyone for their effort. If you are not good enough, then you've just got to say fair enough, learn the lessons and tip your hat to the opposition.

'My biggest disappointment is that this group of players is too talented and too good to go down in history as being a bunch of players that lost a series 3–0, but it has happened and we have got to get on with it.'

That's exactly what the All Blacks were planning on doing. There were still a Tri-Nations and a Grand Slam tour to be won.

Sir Clive Woodward (above) was sent back to England frustrated and embarrassed.

FERGIE McCormick is rugby union royalty. Terms like 'tough-as-nails' and 'mongrel' could have been penned specifically for the Canterbury and All Blacks fullback of the 1960s and early 1970s. McCormick would readily tell any new All Blacks that came into the team during his six years and 44-game stint in the side that to wear the jersey with pride they would have to be ready to 'piss blood' for it. He — and many of his teammates — were 'body-on-the line' types. So when 'Fergie' speaks in Canterbury, the locals listen.

The press don't often call. Normally he's only the first point of contact after an All Blacks team has been accused of being 'passionless'. Or, God forbid, 'soft'. But in 2005 the phone rang after Daniel Carter had surpassed McCormick's then world-record 24 points against Wales when he played fullback for the All Blacks in their 33–12 win at Eden Park in 1969. Carter had scored two tries and kicked five conversions and two penalties to amass 26 points as the All Blacks routed Wales 41–3 to secure their first win on the All Blacks' Grand Slam tour.

'There is no one better than Daniel Carter,' McCormick told *The Press*. 'Let's be honest, he is a superstar — he does everything. He is just a natural footballer, he has got the X-factor. There is never too much hoo-ha with him. You can see he does things right, whether he plays at first-five, second-five or full-back. He gets on with it. You get a lot of these "mirror boys" but he is not one of them. He is just Daniel Carter from Southbridge.'

A boy from Southbridge could retire after a compliment like that . . . but Carter was only just getting started again. The test in Cardiff was his first test back in black after he'd broken his leg in a test against the Wallabies three months earlier — X-rays on the injury immediately after the test confirming a broken fibula in his left leg, as well as significant muscle and tissue damage. Indeed, his Tri-Nations campaign had lasted only 148 minutes — 80 minutes in the bring-us-back-down-to-earth 22–16 loss to the Springboks in Cape Town first-up out of the Lions

After the Lions, came Bledisloe Cup and Tri-Nations success: the trophies paraded by Joe Rokocoko, Doug Howlett and Leon MacDonald.

series, and 68 minutes in Sydney helping direct the All Blacks to a 30–13 triumph.

Leon MacDonald — the converted fullback — filled in for Carter at first-five for the remainder of the tournament as the All Blacks registered a 31–27 win against the Boks in Dunedin and beat Australia in Auckland 34–24 on their way to claiming the Tri-Nations title for the first time in the Graham Henry era.

There was little time to celebrate, however, as the All Blacks eyed the country's first Grand Slam since Graham Mourie's side achieved it in 1978. Henry included five new caps in the squad which would contest tests against Wales, Ireland, England and Scotland. Locks Jason Eaton and Angus Macdonald, prop Neemia Tialata, flanker Chris Masoe, and utility

In 2005, the All Blacks achieved the Grand Slam for only the second time in its rugby history. These are the men that got the job done on one of rugby's toughest tours of duties.

Backs: *Daniel Carter (Canterbury)*, Jimmy Cowan (Southland), Rico Gear (Nelson Bays), Doug Howlett (Auckland), Byron Kelleher (Waikato), Luke McAlister (North Harbour), Leon MacDonald (Canterbury), Aaron Mauger (Canterbury), Mils Muliaina (Auckland), Ma'a Nonu (Wellington), Joe Rokocoko (Auckland), Sitiveni Sivivatu (Waikato), Conrad Smith (Wellington), Isaia Toeava (Auckland), Tana Umaga (Wellington, captain), Piri Weepu (Wellington).

Forwards: John Afoa (Auckland), Jerry Collins (Wellington), Jason Eaton (Taranaki), Carl Hayman (Otago), Andrew Hore (Taranaki), Chris Jack (Canterbury), Sione Lauaki (Waikato), Richie McCaw (Canterbury, vice-captain), Angus Macdonald (Auckland), Chris Masoe (Taranaki), Keven Mealamu (Auckland), Anton Oliver (Otago), James Ryan (Otago), Greg Somerville (Canterbury), Rodney So'oialo (Wellington), Neemia Tialata (Wellington), Mose Tuiali'i (Canterbury), Ali Williams (Auckland), Tony Woodcock (North Harbour).

back Isaia Toeava were all selected for the first time.

Much attention was focused on Carter ahead of the opening test against Wales. He'd only had limited time in the Canterbury jersey to regain his touch, but backs coach Wayne Smith had no problems promoting Carter so quickly. 'The break wasn't a bad one, it wasn't displaced, so he recovered pretty quickly from that,' Smith said. 'He was straight back into it. In the Auckland Ranfurly Shield game, he made 21 tackles and ran the game brilliantly. He's a pretty calm customer, nothing much flusters him and I think he'll step up. He's still developing his game in many ways, even though he's got the skills and the toughness. I'd expect to see him play well at the weekend and keep developing in the next few years. To be a truly great player you have to work on your strengths. He's got a lot of them, but we don't want to heap too many expectations on him. He can't play like he did in the second test [against the Lions] every week.'

Well, he could: his 26 points confirming that his

performances against the Lions were closer to 'commonplace' than 'every now and again' — not bad against a Welsh side which has been unbeaten in eight tests on the way to winning the Six Nations earlier in the year.

Refreshingly there were no excuses from the Welsh camp after the 41–3 mauling. Coach Mike Ruddock — without six of his Grand Slam-winning side, including Gethin Jenkins, Ryan Jones, Dwayne Peel, Gavin Henson, Tom Shanklin and Martyn Williams — preferred to heap praise on the Men in Black. 'New Zealand were far superior on the day. They won the test match very well, they won it easily in the end, but how we progress from here is the key. You will get no excuses from this camp. We were not good enough on the day. We didn't deliver the performance we wanted. The All Blacks are a great team and if you don't deliver you are going to get burned, you are going to get hurt. I am very disappointed at the margin. Once you let New Zealand get the first one in and you are not accurate with your catch-up rugby they will come back and punish you again. New Zealand won the collisions in the contact area and that put them on the front foot. Carter is a very fine footballer and he keeps getting better and better. He put us into the corner when he needed to, got the backline going when he needed to, took the ball up when he needed to. He is a great player.'

Confidence was clearly high in the All Blacks camp. Henry rotated Carter (with Nick Evans) as well as the rest of the team: Mils Muliaina (with MacDonald), Rico Gear (with Doug Howlett), Joe Rokocoko (with Sitiveni Sivivatu), Conrad Smith (with Ma'a Nonu), Tana Umaga (with Aaron Mauger), Byron Kelleher (with Piri Weepu), Rodney So'oialo (with Mose Tuiali'i), Chris Masoe (with Richie McCaw), Jerry Collins (with Sione Lauaki), James Ryan (with Ali Williams), Chris Jack (with Jason Eaton), Carl Hayman (with John Afoa), Anton Oliver (with Keven Mealamu) and Neemia Tialata (with Tony Woodcock).

The mass change had no effect on proceedings:

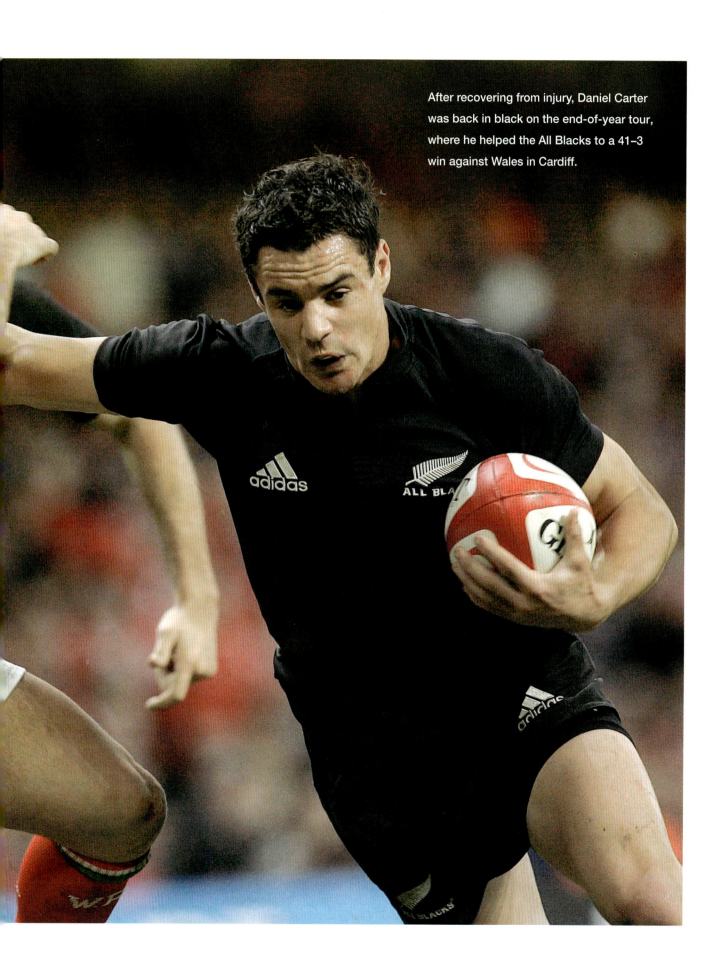

After recovering from injury, Daniel Carter was back in black on the end-of-year tour, where he helped the All Blacks to a 41–3 win against Wales in Cardiff.

the All Blacks cruising to a 45–7 win — two tries apiece to Sivivatu and Howlett, another to Weepu and 20 points from Evans's boot getting the job done.

The next week in England, the selection roundabout continued, with Henry finally settling on his most potent XV. Sivivatu and Howlett formed a back three with Muliaina; Umaga and Mauger linked in midfield, with Carter returning to first-five outside Kelleher. Mealamu started at hooker, while Woodcock and Hayman completed a front row which was locked by Williams and Jack. McCaw — the captain in Dublin — joined Collins and So'oialo in the back row.

Carter was very much the star of the show when the team got to London. He was mobbed by Fleet Street's journalists, who had ordained him as the game's biggest star. Carter was unfazed by the personal plaudits that were coming his way. 'Everyone has their own personal opinion but I don't read too much into that sort of thing. The guys I'm playing around are playing particularly well and that makes it easier. I know I have to do my best for the team and that's what counts,' he said. 'I don't think [the fame thing] is that bad. There's a lot more attention when I go out now but I don't want it to change my life. People ask for autographs but I'm happy with that. It only takes 20 seconds and you can make someone's day. New Zealand is pretty good really, they respect your space [there].'

Carter was pumped for the test against England. With Scotland potentially offering up the easiest game on tour the following week, the Grand Slam effectively lay on the Twickenham date. 'It's the biggest test on tour so far, so the boys are pumped up. We realise it isn't going to be easy because the England team played pretty well beating Australia last week. [England first-five] Charlie Hodgson's playing some pretty good footie at the moment. He's running the show well and they have a really solid midfield with Mike Tindall back. They definitely have some backs who are really dangerous, they also have some very big, strong forwards and will be looking to utilize them.'

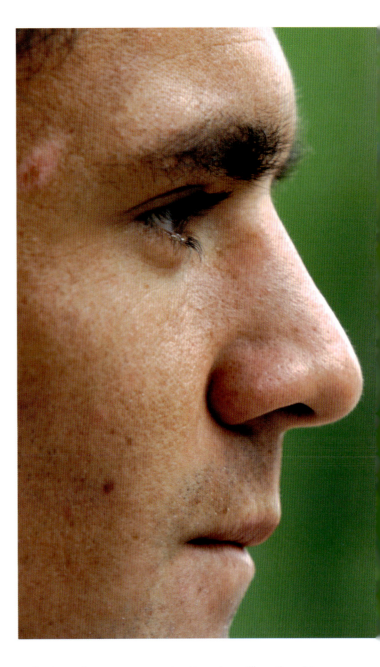

Carter, of course, was looking to utilize the All Blacks' X-factor via the likes of Umaga, Howlett and Sivivatu. 'The expectation is always going to be there but it isn't something I dwell on. You really want to give these guys the ball and give them space so they can weave their magic but you can't just throw them the ball and then expect them to do something. It's up to 14 guys to get the 15th man over the line.'

Carter — who would kick 13 points — lived up to the pre-match hype, leading the team to a 23–19 win. Said England boss Andy Robinson after the test:

> '**I don't think [the fame thing] is that bad. There's a lot more attention when I go out now but I don't want it to change my life.**'

'Dan Carter has everything. He runs the game well and is an awesome goal kicker. He's the best 10 in the world . . .' Both of the All Blacks tries — to Umaga and Mealamu — came from Carter breaks. He, and the All Blacks, were at the top of their game.

So much so that only Umaga, McCaw and Jack retained their positions for the Murrayfield test. And fittingly, in Umaga's last test, the All Blacks won the Grand Slam courtesy of a 29–10 win. 'We came over here to do a job and that was to develop players and also to try to win a Grand Slam,' enthused Henry.

'That was at the back of the players' minds and we'd talked about it. We managed to win the Grand Slam. We played Welsh and Irish sides which had a number of senior players missing. We had a big game against England and we managed to hang in there and win. We faced a very competitive Scottish team and won.'

Forwards coach Steve Hansen was thrilled so many players were used on the tour. 'To do the Grand Slam with 35 players is a huge bonus. What we wanted to do was have faith in people to do a job and they've done that. We'll all form an opinion on whether we've got two players for each position. I think as selectors we're very happy with the performance of people on this tour. There are obviously one or two people still at home, but you can be happy when you finish a test match with the guys we had on the pitch against Scotland and still get the job done. There were some young men out there like Jason Eaton for example. He's had a good tour and developed as a person. Andrew Hore is another developing player. They've both said they want to be All Blacks for a long time and we're very happy about that.'

It's difficult to imagine that anyone in world rugby was happier than Carter at the end of the year. First came the International Rugby Players Association's Player of the Year award. 'It means a lot when you are recognized by the guys you compete with,' said Carter who edged out McCaw for the honour. 'I'm honoured of course, but really have to acknowledge the guys I play with. We make it happen together.'

Then, a few days later, the International Rugby Board's Player of the Year gong was his too. 'It's been a pretty big year and I feel pretty humble to receive an award like this,' he told Radio Sport. 'There have been some great names that have gone before me, so it is something very special to me. I can tell you I was more nervous going up there to receive the award than I get before a test match. There are a lot of people here, it's a great night.'

Early in 2006, the awards kept coming. He was

named New Zealand's Player of the Year for the second year in a row, becoming the first player to win the prestigious Kelvin R Tremain Memorial Trophy twice. And then rugby's bible, the *Rugby Almanack*, named Carter as their Player of the Year. 'It's proving difficult to find flaws in his game,' the editors, Clive Akers and Geoff Miller, wrote. 'Only the factor of time is required before the term "great" can be used.'

YOU can trace the demise of the All Blacks' 2007 World Cup campaign to a famous date: September 11. That was the day in 2006 when the word 'reconditioning' was added to the New Zealand rugby vocabulary. The rugby nation had already become aware of 'rotation', but this was one step further. A step that Graham Henry's All Blacks would never recover from.

The bizarre plan would see 22 All Blacks rested from the first half of the 2007 Super 14. A desperate NZRU board rubber-stamped the deal on 25 May, despite the knowledge that the move would be controversial on so many levels. From a business point of view it was flawed, because it meant crowd numbers and television ratings would fall without the best players in the competition. And while sponsors frowned at the move, senior rugby identities were warning that any move to protect the country's best players would backfire. 'It won't work,' warned Laurie Mains, the last All Blacks coach to lead the team to a World Cup final. 'Rotation won't work because teams are only successful when they play together for long periods. Graham Henry never picks the same test team on consecutive weekends. And reconditioning won't work because the players will be joining the competition behind the eight ball. They'll be playing catch-up and that's when players start taking short cuts. And the only thing that leads to is a loss of form and injuries.'

Daniel Carter bursts through the English defence at Twickenham to set up the first try in the All Blacks' 23–19 win.

The announcement was made just before the All Blacks began their domestic test season with games against Brian O'Driscoll's Ireland, and Argentina. Those games were controversial enough, because Henry had two separate test squads: one for the Irish tests in Hamilton and Auckland, and one which would play in Buenos Aires seven days later.

It was an extraordinary time in New Zealand rugby. Henry, though, was in a bullish mood. His All Blacks had just completed arguably the team's most impressive year since New Zealand played its first international in 1903. And in the just-completed Super 14, New Zealand's dominance was on show again as the Crusaders and Hurricanes played out the competitions final.

Daniel Carter — one of only five Crusaders to play in all 15 games, along with Reuben Thorne, Wyatt Crockett, Greg Somerville and Corey Flynn — had been at his brilliant best throughout the competition. And when halfback Andy Ellis tore a medial ligament in his right knee in the semi-final win against the Bulls, Carter was asked to cover the No. 9 position in the final, in case Kevin Senio was injured. 'He's actually got a pretty good skill set for halfback,' Senio said. 'And he's pretty familiar with all the moves . . . he tells me what to do all the time! This week it's been a good chance for him to get in there and work the forwards [at training] although we're hoping it doesn't happen on Saturday.'

It didn't happen, but if it did, we'd probably have missed it as Jade Stadium was fogged in for the final. The lack of visibility created an at-times farcical affair. Conditions worsened as the match wore on, and sections of the crowd in the multi-storeyed Western Stand were forced to leave the ground because they couldn't see the field, while television coverage was

Not even the fog in the 2006 Super 14 final could stop Daniel Carter and the Crusaders cruising to victory against the Hurricanes.

The All Blacks team was split ahead of the opening tests of the 2006 campaign; Daniel Carter missing the Irish test to play the Pumas in Argentina.

also adversely affected. The conditions ruined what many had predicted would be a quality spectacle between two in-form teams laden with All Blacks. Instead it was a stop-start affair, marred by handling errors and an inability of players to field numerous kicks cleanly. The Crusaders, beaten just once during the season, claimed the final 19–12 thanks to a stellar effort from their forward pack, a try to centre Casey Laulala, and 14 points from Carter.

Carter winged his way to Argentina after the final, along with fellow starters for the Puma test Leon MacDonald, Rico Gear, Scott Hamilton, Isaia Toeava, Sam Tuitupou, Piri Weepu, Mose Tuiali'i, Chris Masoe, Ali Williams, Jason Eaton, Jerry Collins, Anton Oliver, Tony Woodcock and Somerville. The rest of the All Blacks squad — which included the likes of senior pros like Richie McCaw, Chris Jack, Byron Kelleher,

Aaron Mauger, Doug Howlett and Mils Muliaina — remained in New Zealand for the Irish tests.

Predictably, the All Blacks would struggle to reach any great heights in any of the tests. The first, in Hamilton, was won 34–23 and is remembered most as the coming-out party for the team's new skipper. McCaw's teammates gave an insight into his leadership style after they reeled in what was an eight-point deficit with 25 minutes remaining to extend their unbeaten record against Ireland to 19 tests, dating back to 1905.

Muliaina said McCaw kept his head, calling on his teammates to maintain the positive attitude that had got them into trouble in the first half, but to add a couple of tactical tweaks. 'We were under the sticks a few times during the game, and Richie just kept saying that we need to focus on the next job ahead,'

Muliaina said. 'We didn't want to go into our shells but we still had to change the game plan. We felt we were running it and losing the ball in our own half.' And Mauger — playing outside Luke McAlister at first-five — said he witnessed a blunter McCaw message in the changing room at halftime. 'I overheard the forwards talking about rectifying that problem — to get in there and start smacking them around. To their credit they did.'

In the second test things didn't go much better, despite a 27–17 scoreline in their favour. Still, forwards coach Steve Hansen was convinced the stumbling start to the season would prove to be more valuable than romps against the likes of Fiji, Tonga or an under-strength side from Europe. 'We got plenty out of it,' he said of the series. 'Every game's helpful; you learn things all the time. The first game was a bit stuttery because of lack of time together. And [in the second test] the weather didn't help. Even so, there were lots of lessons learnt. People were put under pressure, which is different pressure to Super 14 rugby.'

One of those players was McAlister, who Henry and Co. were keen to groom as Carter's back-up. But his performances were inconsistent — some genius, some naivety. He was one of 11 players flown to Argentina to back up the other 'squad'. And, somewhat ironically, the Buenos Aires All Blacks produced the worst performance of the winter as they struggled to a 25–19 win.

The lack of cohesion led to a crisis meeting between the team management and players before the start of the Tri-Nations. The team was called to Wellington, where Henry laid down the law and demanded more application and dedication from his charges. The team, with no Tana Umaga to rule with an iron fist, had lost its way, but the timely and initially unplanned intervention was a masterstroke from the team's manager Darren Shand, Henry, Hansen and Wayne Smith.

The opening Tri-Nations test — against the Wallabies in Christchurch — pitted Carter against the great Australian No. 10 Stephen Larkham for the first time at test level. And Carter, who had only ever played at second-five-eighth in a test against Larkham, couldn't wait to lock horns with the 1999 World Cup winner. 'Larkham's playing really well and he's got a bit of game time under his belt now after some injuries so he's growing in confidence. He'll be a real threat,' Carter said. 'He and [halfback] George Gregan are experienced guys and they know how to set a backline on fire. They've got the outsides with the ability to do that so we're very aware of their attacking abilities.'

The love-fest was mutual — Larkham saying pre-test that, unlike Carter's All Blacks and Crusaders predecessor Andrew Mehrtens, the Wallabies would get little joy trying to expose him in defence. 'He's a good defender as well,' Larkham said. 'Merhts was always my No. 1 pick, especially in attack; he had his faults in defence occasionally, but Daniel Carter has a full repertoire in attack and defence.' And Gregan got in on the act too: 'Steve I get to watch from a nice part of the field and Dan Carter is good to watch when you're doing your analysis but he's a tough bugger to play against . . .'

Those comments were being made as a backdrop to some extraordinary quotes from Irish coach Eddie O'Sullivan, who had doubled as one of the Lions assistant coaches in 2005. He questioned Carter's ability, saying the Cantabrian had been guided through the formative stage of his test career by Umaga, whose retirement would leave the then 24-year-old without guidance at the top level.

Henry and McCaw jumped to Carter's defence. 'It's amazing the knowledge of some of the coaches around the world about teams they don't coach,' Henry said. 'When [Larkham] was 23–24, he probably had guys outside him — who talked to him. I think it's natural that guys grow in the job. I think Daniel Carter's a fabulous rugby talent and I've got a huge amount of time for him as a person. If he's the finished article now, I'd be very surprised.' And McCaw, making

The All Blacks continued their domination against Australia in New Zealand in the opening test of the 2006 Tri-Nations — much to the displeasure of Stephen Larkham and George Gregan.

the point that Carter was 2005's International Rugby Board's Player of the Year, said his mate had proven his development as someone who could control a game. 'In the last 18 months he's really taken over that. He's got Mauger there as well, who's played a fair bit of rugby. Those two work pretty well together. In those positions you have to run the game, and those two do it pretty well. As time goes on they'll get better and better but they're not bad at the moment.'

And neither were the All Blacks — their early season woes confined to the past with a 32–12 win against the Wallabies. Carter had a good game, too, but if he was looking to send O'Sullivan a message he would do it

in the All Blacks' next outing against the Springboks in Wellington. He kicked 25 of New Zealand's points with a nine-from-nine record in their 35–17 win, and his twin bursts of genius to set up their two tries were impossible to ignore. It all seemed so far away when his first touch was a charged-down punt which saw Springbok halfback Fourie du Preez score a try inside 20 seconds. 'It was a bit of a horror start but as soon as I was back at halfway, I was looking at the rest of the game, trying to implement the game plan and just forget about it,' Carter said. 'Things came right and looking back on it, it wasn't a bad performance.'

Carter got his own back on Du Preez in the last

Daniel Carter skips away from Bok wing Breyton Paulse in the 35–17 win in Wellington.

act of the first half, in a sequence that showcased why the 24-year-old was widely regarded as the rugby world's most valuable commodity. He drilled a monstrous 80-metre punt down the centre of the ground, to which Du Preez responded with an effort of about half that distance. Carter fielded the kick, stepped the Springboks No. 9 without breaking stride to set in motion Weepu's crucial try. 'They're a pretty frustrating team to play against because they do shut down your time and get up in your face,' Carter said. 'They're a different team to most teams we come up against. They put you under pressure. They feed off our mistakes. In the past we've kept them in the game through mistakes.'

Williams — the All Black lock — summed up the value of the team's No. 10. 'The guy doesn't talk, doesn't hype himself up, he just goes about his business. Once you think he's not even on the paddock he'll go and do something. The guy's amazing, controls the game. The individual flair is just huge. Priceless.'

The master-class continued in Brisbane in the team's next outing when Carter nailed a dropped goal, a penalty and a conversion of Joe Rokocoko's try to seal a 13–9 win at Suncorp Stadium. And a further 19 points came in the third Bledisloe test in Auckland in a 34–27 triumph before the team's attention turned towards winning in South Africa. With two tests to play — in Pretoria and Rustenburg — the All Blacks,

The Bledisloe Cup and Tri-Nations were the All Blacks' again, following the 34–27 win against the Wallabies at Eden Park.

who had already claimed the Tri-Nations title, were desperate to get at least one victory over the Boks in the Republic. And they got it first-up, courtesy of a 45–26 win at Loftus Versfeld, before losing their unbeaten 2006 record in Rustenburg when a last-minute error from So'oialo handed the Boks a 21–20 victory.

Still, a year out from the World Cup, the team had played some impressive rugby. But, before the end-of-year tour to England, France and Wales, there was a reminder of 'reconditioning' when the 22 players who would miss the first half of the 2007 Super 14 were named.

These are the players who were selected for Graham Henry's controversial 'reconditioning' programme:
Forwards: Jerry Collins (Wellington), Jason Eaton (Taranaki), Carl Hayman (Otago), Andrew Hore (Taranaki), Chris Jack (Tasman), Richie McCaw (Canterbury), Chris Masoe (Wellington), Keven Mealamu (Auckland), Anton Oliver (Otago), Greg Somerville (Canterbury), Rodney So'oialo (Wellington), Reuben Thorne (Canterbury), Ali Williams (Auckland), Tony Woodcock (North Harbour).
Backs: *Daniel Carter (Canterbury)*, Byron Kelleher (Waikato), Leon MacDonald (Canterbury), Aaron Mauger (Canterbury), Mils Muliaina (Waikato), Joe Rokocoko (Auckland), Sitiveni Sivivatu (Waikato), Piri Weepu (Wellington).

'Many of our best athletes have played several years of continuous rugby without a chance to really get their bodies right,' Henry said. 'The conditioning programme is important for their well-being in the long term and also important to our chances of winning the World Cup.' The coach emphasized that participation in the conditioning programme did not guarantee a place in the World Cup squad. 'We have included 22 of our leading players in the conditioning programme, but there are no guarantees. There is a long way to go before we name the World Cup squad and a large group of players are pushing for selection. The door is definitely open.'

The announcement ensured there was plenty of criticism of the All Blacks coaches on the tour. All of sudden the results weren't as important as they once were. The All Blacks would win all four tests — beating England 41–20, France 47–3 and 23–11, and Wales 45–10 — but the focus was on the rotation: 10 changes from test one to two, five changes from test two to three, and eight changes from test three to four.

At least Carter had the ability to unify the pro-Henry brigade and the growing anti-rotation and reconditioning voices. The occasion was the second French test at Paris's Stade de France. In the build-up to the win, Wayne Smith described Carter as 'probably the best we've ever had' to wear the first-five-eighth jersey. And those words proved prophetic, as Carter controlled a stop-start match and brought it to life with some scintillating breaks and notched up a points-scoring record along the way. 'Daniel is just Daniel, isn't he?' Smith said. 'He was dangerous again. He kicked well tactically when he kicked, and his defence was good again, so he had a pretty good day. He gets his confidence from the knowledge that he does his work. He never takes short cuts. On a Wednesday after a big test match he may be really sore but we have about an hour and forty minute kicking session — he still goes through all the drills and all the kicks.'

Carter's 13 points gave him 56 for the tour (with one test remaining) and a total of 170 this year — allowing him to scrape ahead of the 166 scored by Andrew Mehrtens in 1999. After the Welsh test the following weekend, his total would be 186. It was a positive end to a contentious year . . . although things were about to take a turn for the worse.

WITH the Super 14 written off — the 'reconditioning' programme ensuring no New Zealand team was in

> 'The conditioning programme is important for their well-being in the long term and also important to our chances of winning the World Cup.'

the final for the first time in the competition's 12-year history — attention in 2007 was completely and totally focused on the World Cup.

And at the crucial moments which would determine the All Blacks' status in the tournament, their 'go-to' guy was sidelined. Injured. And, eventually, broken.

Daniel Carter would look back at the World Cup — and New Zealand's shock quarter-final exit — with a heavy heart. Carter would talk of New Zealand's obsession with winning the World Cup for the first time since 1987 as a 'burden'.

'Since winning in '87, we have been expected to win every other World Cup,' Carter told the English newspaper *The Times*. 'That becomes quite a burden, a real weight on your shoulders. There's always that pressure and it is part of the reason some of the guys

I was vulnerable. Not having had a bad experience beforehand, I hadn't a chance to learn from it. It wasn't arrogance; it was just that I hadn't the benefit of what comes from a huge loss. I hadn't played in the 2003 semi-final [loss to Australia]. As long as I learn from this, I think things will be fine.'

Just as in 2003, things looked fine for the All Blacks going into the World Cup. The French had sent a 'C' team to New Zealand for the June internationals and they were dispatched with ease. Canada, never a threat, conceded 10 tries in Hamilton — three of them scored by Carter. In the Tri-Nations, the All Blacks beat the Springboks three times and the Australians twice. The only hiccup came in Melbourne when the Wallabies got home 20–15.

At the World Cup, the All Blacks had a ridiculously easy pool. Games against Italy, Portugal, Scotland and Romania would have been — if the rugby gods had been on their side — followed by a quarter-final in Wales against Argentina, a semi-final against England, and a final against either France or South Africa in Paris.

Of course, the French hadn't counted on losing to Argentina in their group play, which meant Graham Henry's All Blacks would play Les Bleus in Cardiff. Given his team's record in their pool, Henry was confident that all of his cards were falling into place.

come over here. They play over here for a club. You might play more games than you would play in a New Zealand season, but it is more structured. You play for one team, week in, week out, and you are allowed to concentrate on that. In New Zealand, you play for three or four teams; the standard changes but you must always play well.'

Carter revealed that when the team returned to their hotel after the loss against France in Cardiff, he disappeared to his bedroom but found it hard to sleep. He was woken at 4.30 a.m. by teammates Chris Masoe and Ali Williams, who told him to rejoin them for a beer. He said the loss was an enormous personal learning experience after an international career that had been 'plain sailing' until then. 'I thought it would continue like that but it didn't. Looking back, I can see

THE 2007 ALL BLACKS WORLD CUP SQUAD

Backs: Mils Muliaina, Leon MacDonald, Doug Howlett, Joe Rokocoko, Sitiveni Sivivatu, Isaia Toeava, Conrad Smith, Luke McAlister, Aaron Mauger, *Daniel Carter*, Nick Evans, Byron Kelleher, Brendon Leonard, Andrew Ellis.

Forwards: Rodney So'oialo, Chris Masoe, Richie McCaw (captain), Jerry Collins (vice-captain), Sione Lauaki, Reuben Thorne, Ali Williams, Chris Jack, Keith Robinson, Carl Hayman, Neemia Tialata, Tony Woodcock, Anton Oliver, Keven Mealamu, Andrew Hore.

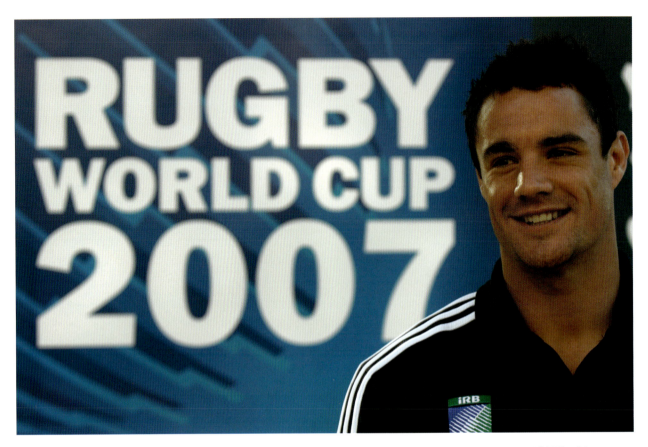

Daniel Carter was all smiles ahead of the 2007 World Cup — just like every other All Black since 1987 had been ahead of the tournament . . .

Certainly the players were confident, even though the pressure valve had been turned up. 'There's added pressure in it being a World Cup,' Carter said ahead of the opening game against the Italians. 'The best players are around, the best teams. It's exciting and you've got to use that energy to play the best that you possibly can. This has been a long time coming for myself . . . and to only be a couple of days away is pretty exciting and I'm looking forward to it.'

The All Blacks burst from the blocks in the tournament with a blistering 76–14 rout of Italy. An astonishing first quarter saw Henry's men race to a 38–0 lead inside 20 minutes. The pace eventually wilted in the heat, but the All Blacks still ended with 11 tries to two against their European opposition. Of course, no one knew it at the time, but the performance against the Italians would not be topped by the team again at the tournament.

The 108–13 win against lowly Portugal was meaningless and error-ridden and, while Scotland were beaten 40–0, the fact that they fielded a 'B' team and the All Blacks struggled with their accuracy and cohesion meant there were plenty of worried frowns amongst the team's management.

And that worry increased ten-fold when it was confirmed that Carter — who'd managed only four from nine kicks at Murrayfield — had a calf strain. It would keep him out of the Romanian game — which would be won 85–8 in another stuttering performance — and the selectors handed the No. 10 jersey to Luke McAlister. It was a strange decision, given that Nick Evans had been Carter's understudy for much of the year and was widely considered 'first cab off the rank' to replace Carter.

After numerous fitness tests in the build-up to the

French dominator Sebastian Chabal seems undeterred by the All Blacks' haka ahead of the team's quarter-final in Cardiff.

quarter-final against France, Carter was eventually passed fit for the game. He would last 55 minutes before being pulled, limping from the field with the scores locked up at 13–13. The substitution coincided with McAlister's reintroduction to the game after he had been sinbinned on the 45-minute mark. Evans replaced Carter, but when he was injured 15 minutes later (with the experienced Aaron Mauger not selected for the game) Isaia Toeava came on for the last ten minutes, with the French leading 20–18. There would be no more scoring action — the All Blacks not even trying a dropped goal when they had the opportunity — and the All Blacks were condemned to bowing out of the tournament in record time.

Carter would speak openly about what went wrong, agreeing his team didn't respond well when the pressure went on in the second half. He said the All Blacks' attack narrowed when McAlister was sent to the sinbin early in the second half, which wasn't their natural game. 'Because we did that, we made it easier for the French to defend against us. Luke came back on and we didn't change our game plan,' Carter said. 'We got our second try from a series of close-in drives, but the French defended a lot tighter after that and we needed to change it, but we didn't.'

Carter admitted his teammates should have attempted a dropped goal. 'This is something we could learn from the England side, and other teams. They have set plays for drop goals. That's a big part of the game over here, whereas you go to the Super 14 and you will probably see two drop goals in the whole competition. We practise drop-goal routines, but it's not part of our culture. In the situation we were in, it would have been the most appropriate thing to do.'

'We practise drop-goal routines,

but it's not part of our culture.

In the situation we were in, it would have

been the most appropriate thing to do.'

Graham Henry asked the public to 'judge me on the World Cup'. Fans did, but the NZRU didn't — and re-signed him through until the end of the 2011 World Cup.

Many thought it would be appropriate, too, for Henry and his coaching team to resign after the All Blacks' worst-ever World Cup performance. They didn't. And remarkably the NZRU reappointed them, despite knowing that decision would send Robbie Deans — the most successful Super rugby coach in history — to the Wallabies.

Carter supported the move. 'When I first got into the All Blacks, Graham was quite an intimidating guy. But once I got to know him, I realized what a great bloke he is. It [the choice between coaches] was extremely tough from my point of view, because I knew that they were both great coaches. You've got to remember, I had worked with them both for years, Robbie Deans at the Crusaders, Graham with the All Blacks. Graham's coaching team of Steve Hansen and Wayne Smith makes him especially strong. Against that, you had Robbie, one of the best coaches I have ever had. I knew it was a win-win situation for New Zealand because there would be a great coach either way. But I also knew we would lose a great coach, whoever lost.

In the end of course it was Robbie and he was a big loss. But he had to coach at international level, it was his time. I think their reasoning behind reappointing Graham was fair. Continually changing the national coach when a World Cup was lost wasn't changing anything. They used the Clive Woodward example of England showing faith in their coach despite failing at the 1999 World Cup. Four years later that loyalty paid off. That's the dream, isn't it?'

Indeed.

Proving that the rugby nation had learnt nothing, the focus after Henry, Smith and Hanson's reappointment immediately turned to the 2011 World Cup to be held in New Zealand. Before the All Blacks would play again, Deans would be farewelled with his record-setting fifth Super rugby title before taking up the Wallabies' reins. Then Ireland and England would be seen off in the domestic test openers in 2008, before the rugby world as we knew it would be turned on its head. Again.

THE MAKING OF THE LEGEND

IT was the best of times. It was the worst of times. And, as ironic as it would be, it was arguably the making of Dan Carter: leader.

The incident itself was as substantial as they come in rugby — a ruptured Achilles tendon ruling him out of rugby for six months at the end of the 2008 season. Ordinarily it would have meant he would miss the 2009 season with the Crusaders. But, of course, Carter was playing for Perpignan at the time of the injury, after being granted leave to play club rugby in France instead of domestic rugby in New Zealand.

That decision was controversial enough on its own, but hindsight tells us that both the decision to play in France and the subsequent injury were something of a blessing in disguise, because Carter, when his return eventually materialized, came back humbled, rested and with the type of steely resolve that would announce to the rugby world that 'DC' was back better than ever.

AFTER the England series was won, Dan Carter held court with the nation's media. The debate had raged for months. Would Carter re-sign with the NZRU, or would he look to cash in on his reputation — and not insubstantial pin-up power — and sign with a European club?

The decision he came to fell towards the latter option, but with a twist. Carter had agreed a six-month deal with Perpignan to play in the 2008/09 French Top 14 rugby competition following the conclusion of his duties on the All Blacks' end-of-year Northern Hemisphere tour. The 'sabbatical' agreed with the NZRU would then see Carter return to New Zealand in June 2009 with an eye on securing his position in the All Blacks through until at least the 2011 World Cup.

Carter had been linked to Toulon for months, and, while he confirmed that he had had discussions with the Tana Umaga-coached club, Perpignan's involvement in the European Cup ultimately convinced him to ink a

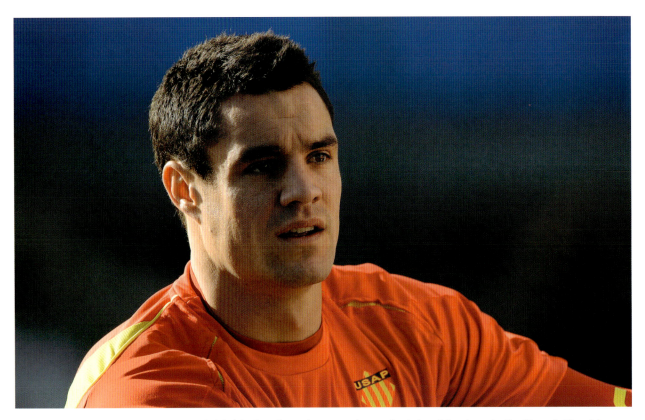

Daniel Carter is pictured (above and right) in Perpignan's two strips as he takes his place in the French Top 14.

deal with the club. 'Obviously we hear a lot about the strengths and weaknesses of the European competitions and how they compare to the Super 14 and the Air New Zealand Cup,' Carter said. 'Basically, if I am going to play rugby in Europe, I want to test myself against the best Europe can offer and I am excited about the challenges both the Top 14 and the European Cup will bring.

'I have done plenty of research on both Toulon and Perpignan and, whilst I have no doubt that I would have enjoyed Toulon, in the end, Perpignan's qualification for next year's European Cup swayed my decision. I would like to thank the NZRU for offering me this unique opportunity. The All Black jersey is no one's by right and I fully appreciate that I will have to continue to play well and prove myself if I am to be involved with the All Blacks next year and beyond. The 2011 Rugby World Cup is going to be a phenomenal event and my priority has always been to be available to take part in that.

'Obviously there is also some disappointment at not being able to be part of the Crusaders [n 2009] and that was probably the hardest part of my decision, particularly given how well the boys finished the season and the excitement around the new coaching structures next year. The Crusaders have been a massive part of my life and I hope that I can continue that association when I return.'

Another reason for picking Perpignan over Toulon was his desire not to be in any shadows cast by Toulon's Umaga or Jerry Collins. 'I [signed with Perpignan] because I didn't want to be surrounded by other New Zealanders. I wanted to test myself, to go somewhere out of my comfort zone, somewhere I wouldn't be able to talk English all the time and relax with Kiwis. That was one of the reasons I wanted to leave New Zealand for a while, to try another lifestyle. I wanted to make new friends and really challenge myself. I felt the only way to do that properly would be to go somewhere there weren't All Blacks. I am

normally a quiet, shy type of person who takes the easy route. This was [going to be a good move for me].'

The All Blacks' sponsors were quick to endorse the deal after a section of the media had, pre-announcement, questioned whether the multi-national would baulk at supporting any move that saw Carter play outside New Zealand. Said New Zealand adidas boss, Greg Bramwell: 'We have been kept fully aware of Dan's intentions from the moment the NZRU offered the chance of an overseas "sabbatical". We have always been very supportive of him taking this opportunity, and reports that we were in any way trying to prevent or impose any conditions on the deal are simply not true. The fact is that it is an exciting opportunity for Dan and we are excited about seeing him back in New Zealand next year and hopefully making a massive contribution to New Zealand rugby through and beyond the 2011 Rugby World Cup.'

Lou Thompson, from Carter's management company Essentially Group, commented: 'This whole process, from the negotiations with the NZRU [led by fellow Essentially Group Director, Warren Alcock, which culminated in Dan signing a contract with the NZRU until the end of 2011, including a sabbatical option] to concluding matters with Perpignan has been uncharted territory for all involved. Whilst everyone had the same goal in mind, there were many steps to take along the way. In some ways we have had to write the book as we have gone along, and I am confident that the agreements that have been reached are good for Dan, Perpignan, the NZRU and ultimately New Zealand rugby.'

Certainly All Blacks coach Graham Henry was convinced Carter's decision would not set a precedent. He said the decision to allow Carter to embark on a short-term stint with Perpignan couldn't and wouldn't be done 'willy nilly. They have to qualify as a long-term All Black who has done a lot for All Blacks rugby. Dan Carter qualified for a sabbatical because he's played a fair amount of time — about six seasons — for the All Blacks. I think senior players who have played a long time for the All Blacks may qualify for a sabbatical and in this case it was pretty important that we keep Dan and it was part of the contractual arrangement, suiting both parties.'

Not everyone was onboard with the decision. An editorial in the tabloid *Sunday News* argued the move was confirmation of a class system infiltrating the All Blacks. 'What else can you surmise from Carter being given permission to join Perpignan for six months? Carter is being treated like no other All Black in history. The NZRU will argue if they hadn't offered Carter a sabbatical he would have been lost to the All Blacks for good. But the truth is if playing for the All Blacks and being paid handsomely for that honour wasn't enough to keep Carter in New Zealand, they should have let him go. No one is irreplaceable. I hope he understands he will be judged harder than anyone when he return to New Zealand. He'll be wearing the black jersey without having done the hard yards in the Super 14 like his teammates. If he wasn't already, DC is now a tall poppy. Good luck with that . . .'

And All Black great Christian Cullen warned lucrative sabbaticals abroad would kill rugby in New Zealand and turn the players into mercenaries. 'I think it's dangerous. You give Dan Carter that, you have to give Richie McCaw the same opportunity, Ali Williams, Mils [Muliaina]. I think it's setting a dangerous precedent. You don't want the All Blacks to become mercenaries where all the good All Blacks are overseas and then they come back and play test matches, because it will kill the game in New Zealand. It's good for the players because they can go and make money, and as we all know, rugby doesn't last forever. But on the supporters' side it's dangerous because the public want to watch the best players in the world. New Zealand could slowly become mercenaries — the

Daniel Carter lines up a penalty for Perpignan against Castres Olympique. The first-five's move to France would be wrecked by injury.

overseas All Blacks come back and play test matches and they're gone. And our domestic competition could be wiped out. Already the NPC is killed in New Zealand. You go to some games and there's 2000 people watching. In the old days mum, dad, son and daughter, everybody's going to be watching it. In the past you could see five, six, seven All Blacks playing against each other in one game. Now, that's not the case. I just don't like the idea. I'm an old sort of traditionalist player. If you play for the All Blacks, you play for the jersey; if you go overseas, you play for that team. If you want to come back, you come back. I don't like the idea of being mercenaries and coming back in and just playing All Blacks and going away. It's going to kill the game.'

Before Carter could pull on the Perpignan jersey for the first time, there was the not-so-small matter of a Tri-Nations and a Grand Slam tour to contemplate.

First up it was the Springboks in Wellington and another battle with his old rival Butch James. And indeed James — never known for his subtle approach — took their rivalry to a new level. But Carter shrugged off the Springbok first-five-eighth's efforts and kicked four penalties and converted the All Blacks' solitary try on the way to a 19–8 win.

After the game, Carter, rather than complain, said that he thought that level of attention was 'natural' if you are a key player in a team. 'It's happened in the past; well, it's just something to expect. I am not too sure of what is behind it, perhaps to put me off my game a bit, but I was able to bounce back. It's just one of those things, a real test match and there is a real tradition behind that and it was played at a really high intensity and it was really physical. But that is just part of the game. It was just the same as any other game against the Springboks, I expect that and it is part of it.'

The first-up Tri-Nations win had been satisfying in what were tough conditions. And Carter felt that for what was basically a new side the All Blacks had played well — especially the forwards, who were under the most pressure to perform against the world champions, and in the absence of skipper Richie McCaw.

'They had to step up and play extremely well, and I think they grew and improved as the game went on and it was very pleasing to play behind a pack like we had. Ali [Williams] did well, obviously it was touch and go whether he was going to play but he got out there and I thought he had a great game.

'And I thought the guys outside me made the most of their opportunities but tactically I was reasonably happy with the majority of the game. The whole backline is looking for space. It starts with the wingers and it gets relayed into myself. I think Ma'a Nonu has really progressed in that area, he has become very vocal and given me a lot of options so that's a great part of his game that has really improved and it's making my job a lot easier.'

But Carter was convinced that the Springboks would go away and lick their wounds and come back even stronger in the second test the following weekend in Dunedin. 'They would have learnt a lot from that game, they played extremely well at home and it was different conditions here. They'll have learnt a lot and they'll come back extremely fired up to have a win before they go home. We really did want to beat the world champions and we were extremely passionate and I thought the Boks started reasonably well and were extremely physical but we played really well for the full 80. I thought we played a lot better in the second half.'

Carter was prophetic, because the Boks played like world champions and won for the first time in New Zealand since 1998 when a late try from Ricky Januarie saw them triumph 30–28. Carter's boot threatened to single-handedly beat South Africa at Carisbrook but he proved he was human with two late dropped goal

The All Blacks — with Daniel Carter kicking 14 points — sneaked home against the Boks in Wellington, 19–8.

misses. And before turning attention to his 50th test, against Australia, which was two weeks away, Carter reflected on a Tri-Nations test that he believed his team let slip. And this time — not surprisingly after a loss — he wasn't so gracious about the treatment severed up to him by the opposition.

'There were still a few situations there and the touch judge and ref picked up a few . . . a bit of off-the-ball play. It is frustrating when you're looking to support after a pass and you're getting knocked over. That happened a few times again but that's just the way they play. They really concentrate on intimidating you physically. It's always been a part of their game, more so than other teams.'

The Springboks' in-your-face approach and the sizzling late try to their halfback proved the difference in the test where Carter kicked 23 points. With the rebuilding All Blacks crossing for just two tries in 160 minutes against South Africa, Carter felt the All Blacks could have overcome it if they hadn't strayed when the heat went on. 'We've got to stick to the game plan a bit better. We can't keep giving them lineouts and easy penalties like we did or else you get punished. We had to keep the ball in play but at times we didn't and that's what they function off — lineouts.'

While Carter controlled another mostly impressive outing for the All Blacks backs, the inexperienced pack lacked authority against a South African forward display vastly improved from Wellington. Locks Anthony Boric and Kevin O'Neill, boasting two caps between them, struggled to combat Victor Matfield at lineout time, while the Springboks' scrum and driving play were streets ahead of Wellington. 'It is a young All Blacks side and we'll learn a lot and look to bounce back from this. The way we played in the second half was a real credit to a lot of new, young faces out there.'

While the All Blacks were licking their wounds, the Springboks were glowing in the spotlight of their historic win. The World Cup, clearly, hadn't quelled their thirst for world rugby domination. 'We're very proud of the World Cup last year,' said Boks skipper Victor Matfield. 'We'll be world champions for four years but that's a competition that's in the past and we need to focus on winning the Tri-Nations.'

Ahead of the first test against the Wallabies for the year in Sydney, the All Blacks were warned by their pivot that they would have to play the game of their collective lives if they were to triumph. Richie McCaw was still not ready to return to the test arena, and Carter knew that the All Blacks would need to be at their absolute best to beat an Australian team that was being led to battle in a Bledisloe for the first time

Daniel Carter (opposite page), attempting a tackle on George Smith, warned that the All Blacks would need to be at their absolute best against an Australian team coached in a Bledisloe Cup test for the first time by Robbie Deans (below). He was right: the Wallabies would win 34–19 in Sydney.

by Carter's former Crusaders mentor Robbie Deans.

As it was, the All Blacks were totally outplayed as they slumped to a 34–19 loss. They gave up four tries in the rout, and the pressure on the team ahead of the return test at Eden Park the following weekend was immense. Carter issued a rallying cry when he told the media that the team would have to play like possessed men if they were going to bounce back against Deans's charges. '[Against Australia] we looked to play a lot more attacking game but when you're dropping the ball as many times as we did you just can't get into the game. When we played with tempo near the end of the first half it looked like the Wallabies were starting to tire, and then through silly mistakes and them being better than us at the breakdown, we just couldn't get our game flowing. The Wallabies are playing with a lot of confidence and playing some good footie. We're going to have to lift our game a hell of a lot if we are going to overcome them next week. We've got a pretty new side and they'll be learning a lot from these experiences, so the more we play together hopefully the better we'll get. Obviously we've taken a hit but we will look to bounce back. The guys who have been around for a while have to step up and hopefully the new guys just follow and add a lot, they bring a lot of enthusiasm. It's just a case of all of us working well as a team. We've just got to be men possessed. We've got to lift another level because [the Sydney mistakes] are not really acceptable at test-match level.'

While Carter and his teammates lifted their levels, there was no doubt that the difference between the two teams in the All Blacks' 39–10 win was the returning McCaw. He put in one of the greatest comeback games from a New Zealand captain, as Graham Henry's side extended the run of losses Australia had suffered at Eden Park. They haven't won at the ground since 1986.

The All Blacks' performance was one of a concentrated application aimed at eliminating the frustrations from Sydney. Ball retention was almost faultless by comparison, while the scrum finally operated efficiently. That gave the inside backs the opportunity to dictate terms. Halfback Jimmy Cowan had clearly his finest game in the All Blacks jersey, while Carter, who landed two conversions and four penalty goals for 16 points, demonstrated the subtleties of his kicking game with a superb display.

Two tries in three minutes at the end of the first quarter to prop Tony Woodcock lifted the All Blacks' confidence. Leading the way with a challenging display was lock Ali Williams, who was in outstanding touch, complementing his control at the re-starts where New Zealand looked so much more assured. He also competed at Australian lineout throws to upset the Wallaby momentum. And McCaw's return in the loose gave a competitiveness lacking in his absence, and his determination eliminated the effect of the Australian loose forwards George Smith and Phil Waugh significantly.

The first try, after 20 minutes, came as the All Blacks spun the ball where second-five-eighth Ma'a Nonu charged at the line. When he went to ground, the All Blacks set up the ruck, and it was Woodcock who positioned himself to take Cowan's pass and batter his way over the line, perfectly slung in low body position. From the re-start the kick was taken, and Cowan sent a kick that rolled towards touch at the corner flag where fullback Adam Ashley-Cooper had no option but to let the ball go out. Williams rose to take the subsequent lineout ball and direct it down to Woodcock, who took the ball again and charged through to score. These were the key moments that ensured the All Blacks' Tri-Nation challenge was worth reinvesting in.

And that investment paid off in the team's next outing in Cape Town against the Boks when the McCaw-and-Carter show again combined to deliver a crucial win against the All Blacks' greatest rivals. Carter may not have taken his kicking boots to Newlands, but he produced a typical piece of class to score the match-winning try over South Africa in the 19–0 win — the first

The All Blacks needed to lift in the return test against Robbie Deans's Wallabies in Auckland, and they did — Daniel Carter, again, leading the way.

shut-out win against South Africa in the Republic.

The All Blacks had been attacking hard with a series of continuity plays that stretched the South African defences before Carter, who had a horror day with his goal-kicking despite registering his 800th point in tests, spied his chance after 64 minutes and broke for the line. He was held just short, but twisted his body and stretched out while on his back to ground the ball under the posts. His conversion, apart from being the first successful goal-kick for either side, gave New Zealand a 12–0 lead. South Africa was soundly out-played and never showed the purpose the All Blacks brought to the match. The Springboks attempted to run the ball, but unfamiliarity led to mistakes under pressure. Then replacement hooker Keven Mealamu couldn't believe his luck when the Springboks tried to run the ball from their own goal-line five minutes from the end. A pass flung by second-five-eighth Jean de Villiers fell into the hands of Mealamu who scored the easiest of tries. Earlier, it was a piece of McCaw magic, a kick into the Springbok in-goal area off his left foot, that set up the try for centre Conrad Smith. It typified another superb game from McCaw, who dominated the loose and saw off rival Schalk Burger early in the second half.

'I remember that game pretty fondly,' says Carter. 'We were under the heat, but still had this really strong belief we could break out in the end and do it. Credit to the guys, that was what happened in the last 20 minutes. It was awesome both to get the win and keep them try-less. We put a huge emphasis on our defence for that game and it really paid off. It was one of the best defensive performances I have ever been involved in.'

With the Wallabies backing up from their earlier 16–9 win against the Boks in Perth with a similarly

Daniel Carter — seen here avoiding the tackle of Juan Smith — produced one of his better running games in the 19–0 win against South Africa in Cape Town.

dominant 27–15 win in Durban, it meant that the Tri-Nations title would come down to the season's third meeting between New Zealand and Australia in Brisbane. And despite the Wallabies suffering a 53–8 loss to the Boks in Johannesburg two weeks ahead of the showdown, a battle royal was expected as the Bledisloe Cup was also up for grabs. And that was what was served up, with Carter hailed as the king in the post-match press clippings.

He would score the vital try in the 28–24 win. And he did it from second-five after Stephen Donald was brought on with 30 minutes to go to replace Nonu. The performance confirmed Carter's status as the premier back in the world game. Carter lent an extra dimension from his new position in the backline, and was able to break through and score the last of the All Blacks' four tries. In the final outcome, the conversions he landed of all of the tries marked the difference between the sides.

'The two trophies meant a lot to the side and the country, and to come back from a couple of early losses in the campaign was a huge relief for the team,' Carter said. 'It was really tough, I thought the Wallabies played extremely well, they played right until the 85th minute and they were always in it. We fought back after being two tries down but there is huge self-belief within the squad and to get a result like that was awesome. The boys were out on their feet, absolutely buggered after that 80th minute when they got that turnover but the way we got back and just 'd'd [defended] up like our life depended on it. [Our defence] was just awesome and at the end of the day that got us over the line.'

Carter was embarrassed to learn that he had done a fist-pump when crossing for his try, admitting that it was a rarity and said the adrenaline had been pumping. 'It was a pretty important part of the game and to get a try was a bit of a rarity but I am not really big on celebrations,' he said. 'I thought Steve brought some real energy and played extremely well. He's a great player and full of enthusiasm. He leads the guys

round the park and he made a real impact, which is what you want your subs to do. He really helped get us home tonight so credit to him, and I enjoyed playing outside him so he definitely added a lot when he came on.'

It wasn't long after the highs in Brisbane when Carter's 'brand' took a hit when he bypassed the chance to play for Canterbury in the Air New Zealand Cup final ahead of the All Blacks' Grand Slam Tour. Canterbury coach Rob Penney wanted Carter to play against Wellington, but Carter — who played in an All Blacks practice game in the week leading up to the final — opted not to play. A frustrated Penney launched a plea for the All Blacks to remain involved in the domestic rugby competition after leading the red-and-blacks to a 7–6 win against Wellington. 'It's important that the best players are seen to be part of it at some point of it,' he said. 'If it's the premier domestic competition then they all need to be available. If you get to this end of the competition it's as hard as any rugby you're going to play. New Zealanders on New Zealanders traditionally has been some of the toughest football. It serves a great purpose for New Zealand rugby and it will be interesting to see what unfolds over the next couple of years and see how it ends up.' Penney had been given access to other All Blacks, including McCaw, during the competition, but he said he was never told why Carter was off-limits.

Eventually Carter would admit the decision was one he made for himself, saying it was a necessary decision given he would be playing for French side Perpignan at the end of the All Blacks tour, which could mean a potential 18 months without rest. 'It'll pay off [in 2009],' he stressed. 'I've had a really good break and I'm ready to go. It's pretty similar to having a good off-season. I've been doing a lot of work on my fitness and physical side of things over the last three to four weeks so I'm in good shape and ready to play test-match rugby again.'

While a few columnists questioned Carter's decision not to front for the province which gave him his break

'I'm in good shape and ready to play test-match rugby again.'

into New Zealand rugby, the drama was quickly forgotten as the All Blacks set off for what they hoped would be a Grand Slam tour via the team's fourth test against Australia in a money-making exercise in Hong Kong.

Certainly Carter was challenged early on when he was handed the No. 12 jersey for the Bledisloe Cup test. With the Bledisloe safely locked away for another year, the All Blacks selectors wanted to try out Donald at first-five from the get-go of a 'big' test.

'It's quite surreal actually,' Carter said after learning of the change. 'It's where I'd played a couple of seasons professionally. It's a new challenge because it has been so long. I'm really looking forward to it. The coaches have made it clear it's not going to be a permanent move, so that's good because I'm probably more suited to the No. 10 jersey, but that 30 minutes in Brisbane when Steve came on, he made a real difference and I think he really deserves his chance at having a start. At certain stages in the game we can swap with our left-foot and right-foot combination. There are certain parts of the field you'd prefer to kick from so we'll be looking at it during the week. I'm not the biggest guy but I'll just have to get into it, I might be a bit sorer than usual afterwards!'

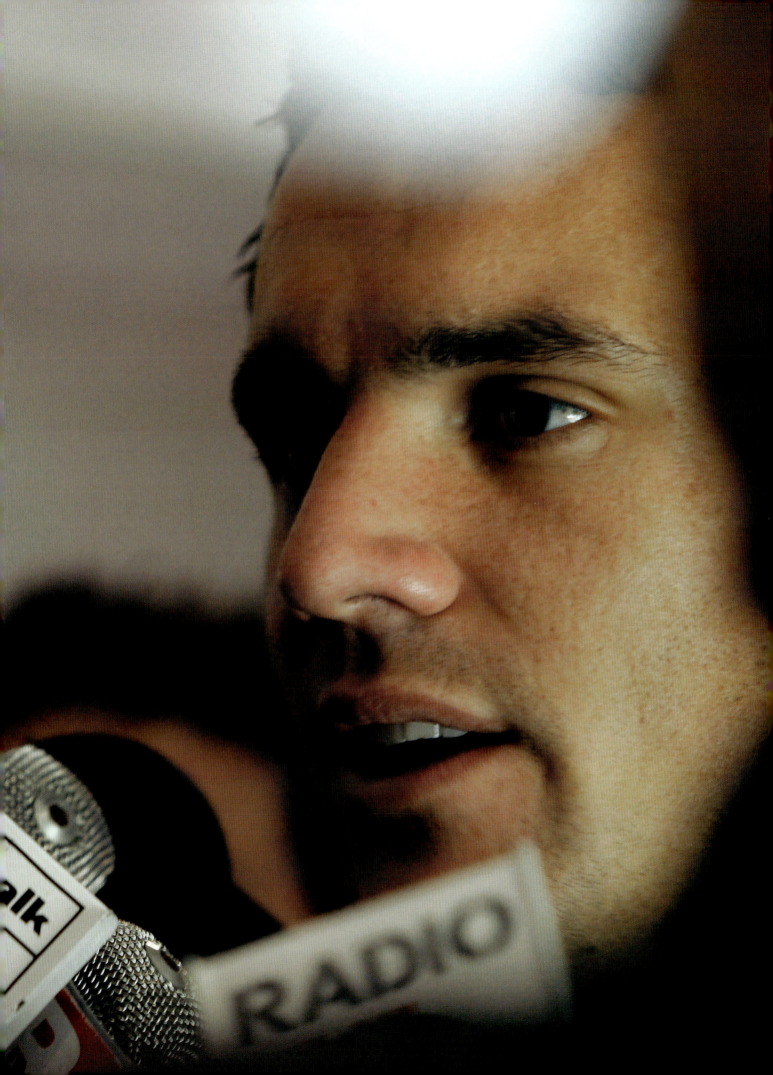

Henry had stressed that the need for 'two navigators' on the field was behind his team selection, but Carter conceded he would have to curb his natural instinct to direct proceedings when operating in the midfield. 'That's something I've been working on all week. Because I'm so used to calling the moves, I need to pull back and let him [Donald] run the show. He's more than capable, he does it extremely well for Chiefs and Waikato, so I just have to sit back and still provide that voice but more from phase play, providing options and let him know what's going on from phase play. I know when I'm playing at 10 if you have a lot of voices providing you options it makes your job a lot easier, so my main role is to make the job as easy as I can for Stephen.'

The tour — with new All Blacks Ben Franks, Hosea Gear, Cory Jane, Jamie Macintosh, Liam Messam, Kieran Read and Scott Waldrom onboard for the first time — got off to a positive if unspectacular start with a 19–14 win over Australia — Carter kicking three penalties alongside tries to McCaw and wing Sitiveni Sivivatu.

The victory left Carter believing the All Blacks were on course for their third Grand Slam after previous successes in 1978 and 2005. 'It is always a tough challenge to go for a Grand Slam and often you do have to grind out wins. We have done that on a couple of occasions now. It is good to know we have that character within the side because it goes a long way when you are not playing as well as you would like. We are having to rely on our grit to get us through in the second half. To have the heart and character in the team is really rewarding. It can get you out of jail.'

Carter also warned Scotland, Ireland, Wales and England that the Tri-Nations champions still had plenty of improving to do. 'It is very satisfying to get through with a win, it sets us up well for the tour,' Carter said in Hong Kong. 'We are not all that happy with the way we played. We are a better side than that, we are much more skilful and still have a long way to improve. We were a bit rusty. We have only

been together for five days so to come out with a win is great and a good step for us. Hopefully as the tour goes on we will get better every week.'

Henry would make 13 changes to the starting line-up that beat Australia for the Slam's first match against the Scots. But not even the introduction of new caps Messam, Read and Mackintosh — and the resting of many of the starting XV, including McCaw, Carter, Conrad Smith, Jimmy Cowan, Rodney So'oialo, Brad Thorn, Jerome Kaino, Andrew Hore and Tony Woodcock — would offer Scotland any real hope of a massive upset.

Indeed, the All Blacks, with Keven Mealamu captaining the team, cruised to a 32–6 win, with Anthony Tuitavake, Piri Weepu, Richard Kahui and Anthony Boric all scoring tries at Murrayfield. None of the try-scorers would be on show a week later in Dublin, though, as the 'A' team was back on duty. And, not for the first time, McCaw and Carter dominated as the Kiwis won 22–3 at Croke Park.

After a rare midweek game against Munster, won 18–16 after a late Joe Rokocoko try, the top All Blacks side was back for what was long thought as being the toughest of the tour's games — Wales at Cardiff.

The Welsh did what they always do pre-test — they talked themselves up. But it was to no avail as the All Blacks' set-piece dominance laid the foundation for the All Blacks 29–9 win. Nonu and Kaino scored the only tries of the game, after 54 minutes and in injury time, respectively. And while the Welsh led 9–6 at halftime, the All Blacks were never in danger of their first loss to Wales since 1953. Carter, who was instrumental with his 19-point haul, admitted some surprise at how well the team had coped since the World Cup loss at the same ground and following the post-World Cup player exodus, which had claimed senior pros like Carl Hayman, Chris Jack and Luke McAlister.

'I'm definitely surprised at how well the team has coped with the players moving overseas. For a new-look side it has been great. We had our backs against the wall with two losses early on in the Tri-Nations but we fought back and won the title, which was superb. Hopefully we can keep working hard and get over that final hurdle against England. It would be a very successful year if we did that. Winning would be huge, going unbeaten on tour has been a real goal that we have been working towards. It would be good to be involved in an All Blacks side that has won two Grand Slams. To do that again would mean a lot to me. We are not trying to build things up because what happened at the World Cup was a bit of a disappointment. It would mean a lot for this team because it is quite a different side to what we had last year. Losing so many players was a little bit daunting but there was excitement over the guys who were coming through.'

One of the most intriguing aspects of the Twickenham test against England was the expected match-up between Carter and the home side's new first-five sensation Danny Cipriani. When he was axed from the test line-up and replaced by Toby Flood, some were left wondering if the extensive press coverage of Cipriani's life on and off the pitch by the British tabloids might have had something to do with it. Carter, when quizzed about his new rival, admitted striking a balance between rugby and 'life' was crucial. 'It would have been good coming up against a young up-and-coming talent, but it's not to be. There is a lot more media attention in the UK; I guess we are quite lucky in New Zealand. While everyone is passionate about rugby in New Zealand, they are keen to leave you alone off the field. It's something I pride myself on. When I'm on the training pitch, in team meetings and playing, 100 per cent of my focus is on that. And I always give 100 per cent.'

One hundred per cent was the record the All Blacks

Daniel Carter was looking forward to locking horns with his England opposite, Danny Cipriani, ahead of the All Blacks test against England at Twickenham. However, the match-up of the first-fives would never eventuate as Cipriani was replaced by Toby Flood.

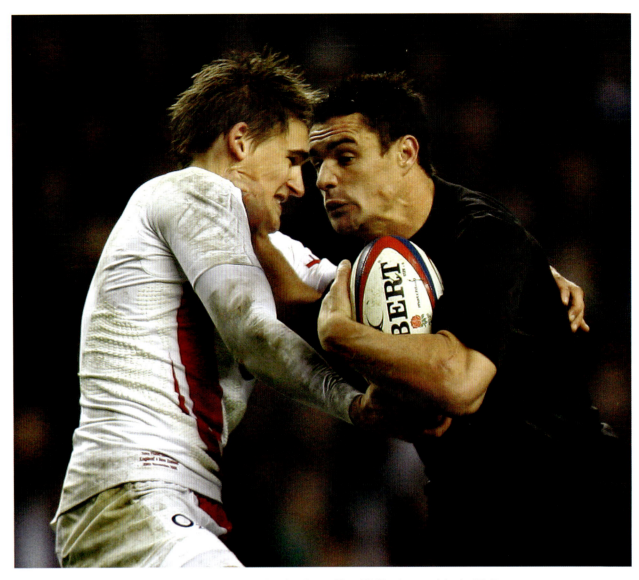

Tony Flood attempts to tackle Daniel Carter at Twickenham. The All Blacks would win 32–6.

would leave Europe with after a 32–6 destruction job on the Poms that set all sorts of records. In achieving the win over England, McCaw's men completed the longest run of victories over England, making it seven in a row since 2004. That beat the six consecutive victories achieved between 1953 and 1972. The All Blacks were also the second side to complete a Grand Slam series without their line being crossed. And the Slam, the third by a New Zealand side, was the eighth achieved by Southern Hemisphere sides following the South Africans in 1912–13, 1931–32, 1951–52 and 1960–61, and Australia in 1984.

And Carter, too, was in the record books as he extended his test-points haul for the season to 203, which broke his record haul for an All Black in a calendar year of 186 set in 2006. Scoring 200 points in a year was previously the domain of All Blacks on tours to Britain or South Africa, when first-class games were also included. Those who have scored 200 points in a year are: Billy Wallace 240 (1905), Don Clarke 218 (1960), Grant Fox 224 (1987), and Carlos Spencer 202 (1997).

It had been some tour. And as his teammates headed home, Carter headed to the south of France . . .

PERPIGNAN. Historically, the last major town in Languedoc before the Spanish border is known, lovingly of course, as 'sleepy'. It's close enough to the Catalan capital Barcelona to be cast forever in the 'little brother' role. Its food and wine are world-famous in Spain, but most headlines dedicated to the town these days concern the clash of cultures between some sections of the Catalan and Romany communities and the fast-growing North African contingent. Indeed, in recent years Perpignan has become a stronghold for Jean-Marie Le Pen's right-wing Front National party which claims that the city's original white inhabitants have been overrun by foreigners from Morocco and Algeria who have moved to France to escape repression in their home countries.

In December 2008, the town was in the news for another reason. Dan Carter — the region's newest fad — would be handed his debut in Perpignan's European Cup tie against England's Leicester Tigers at Stade Aimé Giral. His debut, of course, was highly anticipated by supporters and the international media at large. His arrival at the club was something akin to the second coming — Dan Carter, the club's faithful believed, was the man who would finally deliver the championship success, both domestically and in European competition, that the club had craved since they were beaten by Toulouse in the 2003 European Cup final in Dublin. Perpignan had made it through to the knockout stages for the fourth time in eight tournaments earlier in 2008, before going down 20–9 to London Irish. Carter, they were convinced, was the man to get them over the hump. So much so that in the club store, watches with Carter as a logo instead of the famous Cartier were the biggest-selling item followed by Carter T-shirts, jerseys and his Jockey underpants brand.

'We were obviously bitterly disappointed with the loss last year in the quarter-final,' said Jacques Brunel, the club's director of rugby. 'Although the level of the [English] Premiership is very high — and London Irish are as good as any team in the Division — we had played very well against them in the pool stages and perhaps we ourselves lost the game through our errors. There was a great deal of frustration and that galvanised us in our preparation for this year's campaign. [Carter] will, we hope, provide that little extra which can often make the difference between winning and losing — particularly at this level of rugby — where it is often the small details which are the most important.'

Carter would start his stint with his new club in the best possible way. He kicked 16 points on debut and was named Man of the Match after helping steer Perpignan to a 26–20 win. One of England's great rugby scribes — the Daily Telegraph's Mick Cleary — waxed lyrical about Carter's debut. 'In these times of devaluation, Carter's worth, even at £30,000 a match, shines bright,' he wrote. 'He did miss two straightforward shots at goal either side of half-time, but, hey, no one expects him to walk on water just yet. The miracles can wait. Carter even managed to survive a tip tackle from Harry Ellis. And Ellis somehow survived. At the final whistle, there were backslaps and hugs. The Kiwi boy from far away was already beginning to feel at home. His work has only just begun, of course, and it's almost an impossible task for Perpignan to qualify for the knockout stages. Carter the pin-up boy, Carter the catalyst, Carter the points gatherer, Carter the icon — the lad from the small farming community of Southbridge in rural Canterbury will be expected to play all these roles over the next six months. He has to do no more than be himself, the supreme fly-half in the world game. But he has to make others be more than they presently are. That is the hope. That is the investment. He certainly drew some terrific performances on Sunday from his back row; especially two try Gerrie Britz and openside, Ovidu Tonita.

'No man bigger than the club? Carter had better be. As ever, he looked assured, despite the fact he'd only had 10 days with his new teammates. It didn't take long for him to feature. He may look something of a

Daniel Carter impressed in his early games for his new
team Perpignan, as he began his sabbatical away from
the pressure of New Zealand rugby.

soft touch but he punches his weight in the tackle, flooring Geordan Murphy and Matt Smith in quick succession. He did fluff a high take under pressure but cleared his lines with aplomb. Even if he doesn't quite bring off what he's attempting, he puts defences on edge. A ricocheted kick in the 12th minute was enough to win a penalty when Dan Hipkiss pushed wing, Adrien Plante, Carter landing his first points for the club from 30 metres. Ten minutes later his half-break and inside pass saw Plante high-tackled by Hamilton. Cue another three points. Carter slotted in, and that's to his great credit. Without the ballyhoo, you wouldn't have known it was his first game in a foreign environment. A financial risk? For sure. But it's already paying dividends.'

For his part, Carter hailed his European debut as a 'great start', telling local reporters: 'I'm pleased to have got the first game out of the way. I did feel the extra pressure but the supporters were fantastic and I'm only pleased that I was playing for Perpignan and not Leicester. I'm pleased the way the game went. I thought our defence worked well most of the game though we're disappointed that Leicester were able to cut our lines a few times. I was very pleased that our combinations worked well after just one week together to prepare. It was satisfying that things worked well, though I was disappointed to miss two kicks. I'm just grateful that they were not crucial to the result of the game. To have come and beaten a team of the quality of Leicester in my first game in Europe was a great start. The game was very similar to what I am used to in Super 14. The standard was just as high.' Carter had been fortunate to escape injury after being up-ended by England scrum-half Harry Ellis late on. 'I wasn't injured at all, but it was a bit scary when you find yourself in that position and you have no control over how you're going to land,' he said. 'I was relieved not to be injured.'

Carter would come back to earth soon after when he struggled in his first French Top 14 match for Perpignan. He missed four penalties in a 17-minute

stretch in an unconvincing 16–9 win against Castres. But he was back to his best for the showdown at Stade de France with Argentinean Juan Martin Hernandez during Perpignan's clash with Stade Français in front of 79,122. In its match report, scrum.com reported that, after the 13–13 draw, 'it was clear which of the two pin-up number 10s had won the day. Carter was not at his imperious best but his second-half performance turned the match in Perpignan's favour, allowing them to grab a draw when they were 13–3 down with eight minutes left. Carter, playing only his fifth match for Perpignan, won the points battle eight to six and was a class apart after the break, offloading superbly at times and setting up a key try for Maxime Mermoz late on with a deft dabbed kick.'

Brunel was full of praise for their adopted Kiwi. 'Carter was at ease and was very enterprising,' he said. 'He kicked a little too long at the start of the match but he was able to rectify that. He set things in motion, he provoked and found solutions with his centres. And he made the try with a judicious kick. He is imposing himself more and more on our game and is feeling better and better with this team.'

But there was another paragraph in the match report which would prove the most alarming. 'The All Blacks pivot, who kicked the equalising penalty two minutes from time, ended up limping back to the dressing room with an ankle injury sustained, as it happens, following a tackle by Hernandez but he had made his mark by then.'

A day later the world learnt that Carter would be out of rugby for at least six months with a ruptured Achilles tendon. Said Carter: 'When the injury happened, I heard this rifle shot and looked behind me to try and see who had been the sniper in the crowd. But I felt this really sharp pain in my leg as though I'd been kicked badly. The medics came on to the field and I quickly realized I couldn't push down on to my ankle at all. I had the operation and the surgeon said it was neat and quick, 28 minutes.'

The news meant his sabbatical was over. And it

meant a shiver went down the spine of All Blacks rugby, too. Questions were asked about Perpignan's management of Carter. Before his third game for the club — against Brive — he missed training because of a sore Achilles but passed a late fitness test. After his game against Bourgoin, his fourth for the club, he talked about the injury, saying 'the pain was getting worse after about half an hour and as a precaution I came off at halftime. I'll get tests on Monday and will decide with the staff if it would be better to take several days off from training.' Perpignan's doctor Carlos Vela also told French newspaper *L'Equipe*: 'Dan has not suffered a tear but a slight inflammation of the upper middle of the tendon that primarily requires rest and appropriate care, but there is nothing serious.'

'Experts' up and down the country filled the country's talkback phone lines, questioning whether any athlete had come back with the same acceleration as they had before an Achilles injury. The prophets of doom were put on ice somewhat when eight weeks after the injury All Blacks doctor Deb Robinson revealed that Carter was ready to start walking again. All Blacks physio Peter Gallagher had travelled to France and met Carter in Perpignan, and the news, Robinson told a packed news conference, was all good. 'Pete's very happy with where Dan is at. The wound is looking good, although the calf is obviously wasted because he's been in a moon boot for nearly eight weeks. The very first thing he has to do is normalize his walking gait. When people are in a moon boot and haven't been able to bend and stretch the ankle, they lose their ability to have a normal gait pattern.'

Gallagher spent the next 10 days working with Carter on his rehabilitation programme, which included general as well as specific strengthening work and an aqua-jogging programme. 'Dan tends to his rehabilitation and his personal conditioning in an exemplary way, and works really hard on things he can do,' Robinson said. 'He's been working hard in the gym doing those things, and now we can add in some more upper-body work.'

Gallagher's visit was key to Carter's mental recovery. 'I began to look at life much more positively again. Once I could move again, I turned up to club training. I couldn't participate but I could give some advice to individuals, here and there. We'd talk about the opposition and I'd try to contribute. I still felt part of the team by doing that and it was important. The team have been great to me. They made me feel at home immediately, even though I was the centre of their jokes because I couldn't speak the language. I have made some great friendships here which is the number one thing I love about rugby. The friendships you make in this game last a lifetime and I made those friendships here by staying.'

Robinson was cautious about naming an exact time for Carter's likely return to rugby: 'If things go well, I still think we're looking at around the six to eight months mark for some sort of rugby. Obviously once he gets into running, it's a little bit of how he responds to that. We'll probably be able to count out the weeks a little bit better from that stage. We'd want to see him when he's getting back into rugby-related training. It'd be nice to be able to supervise that.'

Carter's rehabilitation was helped, morally at least, by the success gained by Perpignan in his absence. While European success was a step too far for them, they upset favourites Stade Français 25–21 in the Top 14 semi-final before beating Clermont Auvergne 22–13 to win their first title in more than 50 years.

Despite his injury and lack of on-field experiences, Carter told the *New Zealand Herald*'s Peter Bills that his sabbatical had been something of a life-changing experience, which left him a more mature, more rounded, and less shy person. 'It has really opened my eyes on living in a different part of the world. Further down the track, I could see myself back living somewhere in Europe. I can even see myself spending a lot more time here, perhaps finishing my career. I have so enjoyed it.'

The injury — and time on the sideline — offered him an opportunity to analyse himself and his life, to

'It has really opened my eyes on living in a different part of the world. Further down the track, I could see myself back living somewhere in Europe.'

ponder his past achievements and future goals. Rarely, in these times of professional rugby, does any top-class player get the opportunity of so long a break. Carter has used it wisely. He travelled extensively all over Europe. There had been weekend trips to Paris, plus a few days in places like Monaco, Milan (watching soccer at the famous San Siro stadium), Dublin, Amsterdam and Stockholm. He'd become an avid Barcelona FC fan.

'I have made the most of this opportunity. I have looked back and reflected on my career. People say I have had a good career but you don't think about it. I have had a great time as a professional rugby player, being able to play the game I love and to travel. But to experience another life as I have done in the middle of my career has been fantastic. I take life seriously but I am quite a relaxed guy down here in the south of France and it's easy to become that way. I have been shopping, sight-seeing, things that help make you relax. Punctuality has gone out of the door. I know it will be something I'll have to get back to but I will have time to adjust when I get home. Having this freedom has been good for me. I have been playing seven years of very intense, full-on rugby. But when I got injured, I realised it was an opportunity to take stock, do something different. The main reason I stayed in France was that I already enjoyed the lifestyle of living in Europe. And I've had a great time.'

His extended stay in France also helped him develop a better understanding of what New Zealand rugby means to the rest of the rugby world. 'There is quite a mystique about New Zealand rugby,' he said. 'The people in France want to know what we do differently, why we are different. They all admire rugby in New Zealand; they all think it is the best. They strive to get to that level. There is no doubt there is still something special about rugby there and I am thankful I can be a part of it. For a country that is so small and not many people have heard very much about, they seem to produce this rugby dream, a country that always seems to be at the top of its game. How can such a small country produce a team like this for so many years? Well, there is real history behind the All Black jersey. When you become an All Black, you look at the jersey, you think of the traditions and the people that have gone before you . . . the people you looked up to when you were young. I think what it comes down to is the desire to leave a legacy on the jersey, which means you have to perform in every game. No game is just another game in that jersey. It doesn't matter who you are playing, it is always very special because you know it is going to be such a short time in your career. You have to make the most of that opportunity.'

His decision to stay undoubtedly endeared him to the club and his teammates. Most players in a similar situation would have packed up and rushed home. 'I felt like I had let the club down,' he admitted. 'Part of the reason I was enjoying being here was I didn't find pressure from people generally. The Perpignan supporters are very passionate and there is still pressure on you to perform, with a lot of expectations. But I found that after the match or away from the stadium, I could completely switch off. I couldn't read French newspapers so I found I was able to get away completely from all the hype. I haven't really done any interviews either, so I got away from the media too. I'll be very happy to get back into all this when I get home and start playing, but it was wonderful to be able to get away from it all for some months.'

When asked by the *Herald* days out from his return to New Zealand about whether his heart would remain in Europe or be back home with him, Carter made an unequivocal statement about a possible future conflict of emotions between his homeland and a new life in Europe. 'I would say I have a feel for the two of them now. New Zealand can be difficult at times, but the rewards are so much better. Playing for your country and winning competitions still give special pleasures. Because of the injury, I now want to play again. It's been good here and I have had a great time but I am ready to return to my Kiwi lifestyle. I'm really hungry to play again. There are still major goals I want to achieve. Playing for the All Blacks is still the most important thing for me. There is no way I will turn my back on that. And I think I will always end up in New Zealand eventually. However, having said that, I can definitely see myself spending more time in the future in Europe.'

Any European adventures, though, wouldn't come until, at the earliest, after the 2011 World Cup. And his first tentative steps back towards the dream of guiding his team to its first World Cup since 1987 would come via his Christchurch club Southbridge in a game against Hornby at Denton Oval — a ground which hadn't seen any hype since some cycling events were held there during the 1974 Commonwealth Games. 'I played all my age-group rugby for the club but have never turned out in a senior match for them, so it will be a new experience,' Carter said. 'I'm really happy with where my training is at following my injury. I've done a lot of running in the past few weeks and speed work and contact work this week so I'm confident that I'm ready to go.'

Carter defied predictions by playing all 80 minutes, scoring a try and drop-kicking the conversion to end a match dominated by Southbridge 34–13. Neville Carter, Southbridge's coaching convenor, club committee representative and bar manager, as well as father of the day's main attraction, had the honour of presenting his boy with a club tie for his first senior game. 'This is the first time he's played for them since 2001 when he played in the 125th jubilee game for a Southbridge Invitational team. It was great to see him out here today having a bit of fun.'

Carter junior thought so, too. 'It was a lot of fun. It was good to be back playing some rugby. It's been a long road to getting the boots back on and having a game, so I really enjoyed it. [The Achilles was] no worries at all. It was fine. It was tested a bit on the muddy ground but no problems.'

There were problems, though, for his teammates in the All Blacks. As the All Blacks headed into a two-test series against France and Italy, coach Graham

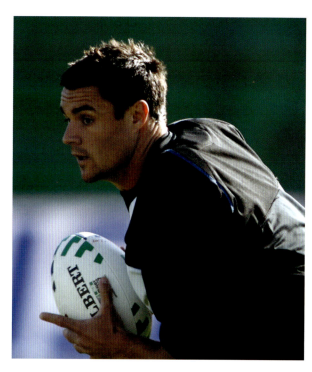

The All Black star felt like he had let his French club down as he headed back to New Zealand to begin rebuilding his All Blacks career.

Henry was convinced there was little chance of Carter adding to his 59 tests in the Tri-Nations, which started after the games against the Northern Hemisphere sides. 'I think that's a very, very outside hope,' Henry said. 'I just think Dan has to make sure he gets himself right. If he feels he's in good nick and can play at international level, he can let us know. But it's a big step, particularly in [his] position where there's a lot of quick movement.' Henry said it would be 'a really big bonus' if Carter was to front, but his real focus ahead of the French and Italian tests was the battle between Stephen Donald and Luke McAlister for the No. 10 jersey.

Both would be involved in the first test of the year, with Donald on the field and McAlister starting from the bench. Other features of the first test side for 2009 against France in Dunedin saw lock Isaac Ross given his debut, while fullback Mils Muliaina became New Zealand's 64th captain, filling in for the injured McCaw. It was, though, a forgettable night as the All

With the influential Daniel Carter and Richie McCaw missing, the All Blacks slumped to a opening loss against the French in Dunedin.

Blacks slunk to a 27–22 season loss. Down 11–17 at halftime, the home team fought back to tie the scores at 17–17, but conceded a penalty goal, and then a 70th-minute intercept try when replacement second-five-eighth Luke McAlister fed the ball to lurking French fullback Maxime Medard, which put paid to the comeback when Medard streaked 50 metres to score. French hooker William Servat asserted after the game that the All Blacks hadn't shown his team any respect immediately before the game. '[The All Blacks] put their headphones on and were smiling a bit. I'm not sure they were smiling after playing against us . . .'

A week later, the All Blacks levelled the series score with an unconvincing 14–10 win in Wellington, but, because of points differential, lost their grip on the Dave Gallaher Cup for the first time. Things weren't much better another seven days on either, when the All Blacks limped to a 27–6 win against Italy — a scoreline that flattered the New Zealanders. Donald was stood down from the No. 10 duties for the Italian test, with McAlister promoted to the role. But he was at best unconvincing and heading into the Tri-Nations the question everyone wanted an answer to was this: 'When is DC back?'

RICHIE McCaw tried his best to be convincing. After two consecutive losses to the Springboks, Dan Carter trained with the All Blacks and, soon after, it was decided that he would play against the Wallabies in Sydney a few days later. When asked what he thought Carter's return would mean to the side, McCaw looked down the camera and offered, 'We don't expect him to come back in and be the miracle man . . .'

Luke McAlister was unconvincing — along with many of his teammates — as the All Blacks struggled to dominate the Italians in Christchurch.

Perhaps McCaw didn't expect it, but, having played enough rugby alongside Carter for Canterbury, the Crusaders and the All Blacks, he certainly wasn't surprised when Carter played the role of hero to perfection.

First, though, the back story . . . Following his game for Southbridge, Carter was drafted into Canterbury's NPC team — something he'd decided would be a long-term thing after turning his back on a $400,000-a-year deal to sign with Auckland and the Blues. Canterbury chief executive, Hamish Riach, said the province was 'absolutely delighted to be able to re-sign Dan until after the next Rugby World Cup. While there has been intense media speculation about Dan's future, our discussions have been positive and constructive throughout and have led to this agreement. Dan is obviously a world-class player and it will be fantastic

to have him back.' Carter, too, was happy that the speculation was over as he looked forward to the rest of the year. 'I'm looking forward to playing in a red-and-black jersey again and being part of the province that has given my rugby so much.'

While Canterbury were celebrating Carter inking his deal, the rugby nation as a whole was upbeat after an opening 22–16 Tri-Nations win against the Wallabies at Eden Park. With Richie McCaw back at the helm, the All Blacks — and Donald — had the last laugh at critics, many of whom had forecast Australia's first win at the ground since 1986. Donald, under massive pressure, landed five penalty goals and a conversion in the game, which saw the New Zealanders play with greater cohesion than at any other time in the winter to that point.

A week is a long time in rugby, though, and while

Carter was preparing to play for Canterbury in its opening NPC game against North Harbour in Albany, the All Blacks were losing 28–19 in Bloemfontein. 'I have turned into the All Blacks No. 1 supporter,' Carter said. 'I get nervous, which is a weird feeling because there is nothing I can do sitting in front of the TV. I just get nervous for the boys because I know all the hard work they will have put in during the week. And I also know it can go either way for them on the field. There is still no harder challenge than playing South Africans in South Africa. It provides a completely different challenge because the crowds are a big factor. They are so hostile, vocal and passionate about their team and the game of rugby. You are told constantly by the South African people you will lose. That can inspire some people or make it harder for other guys.'

On the eve of the All Blacks test in Durban, Carter held centre stage in Albany against Harbour. And despite Canterbury's 22–19 loss, Carter did enough to excite the rugby public. 'I do have mixed feelings,' Carter said after the loss. 'The body's feeling good and it was good to come through unscathed, but it is disappointing to have had a loss like that. I think I've got my speed back, and a little bit of explosiveness and the spring in my step should come in the next month or two. That's been a real positive for me. The rest of the body has a few bumps and bruises because I haven't played for so long but the Achilles is fine and feels strong.'

Carter's contribution to the Canterbury performance, according to veteran rugby scribe Lindsay Knight: 'He kicked four penalties and a sideline conversion of left wing Sean Maitland's first spell try and generally found space with his kicking to show that his potent left boot was not feeling the effects of the injury.'

When the All Blacks' result in Durban filtered through — a 31–19 loss — calls for Carter to be restored to the side grew in momentum. But Carter was doing his best to downplay the chatter. 'My real focus is right here in front of me with Canterbury and I want to keep focusing on one week at a time and playing well. If I

can get three or four games under the belt I guess I'll talk with the AB guys when they get back. I want to try to find some form to get myself back into contention for that black jersey. It is a big step up from this level so I just want to improve from each week.' The soap opera had begun. In Durban, under-fire All Blacks coach Graham Henry told the press: 'We'll watch NPC rugby and see how things are going. We might need a couple of replacements through injury. There'll be no panic. We'll have a look, as we always do . . . Daniel is obviously one of the players we'll look at.' On criticism of the All Blacks' Tri-Nations form, Henry said the team had to 'take it on the chin and do our best. We understand we're judged by past performances and not what we've done in our history. When you lose two test matches and you're not happy about the way you play, you've got to be honest and open and frank about it.' There were three weeks between the Durban test and the All Blacks' next assignment in Sydney. And Springbok captain John Smit was happy to add his thoughts to the conversation about selecting Carter. 'I can't see why not . . . he's a wonderful player. I was probably celebrating his move to France more than anyone. What Dan Carter brings is probably the best in every department. He's not only a good runner. He's a good kicker; he's got a good tactical head on his shoulders.'

On the field, Carter was doing everything right. He scored all of Canterbury's 22 points against Auckland as they grabbed a 22–16 win. His points haul included a decisive try 10 minutes from fulltime — a score that complemented his all-round tactical kicking to add to his five penalties and a conversion. Predictably, after the game, microphones and tape recorders galore surrounded Carter. And, in as much a show of support for All Black incumbent Stephen Donald than anything else, he played down his performances and his chances of playing against the Aussies. 'The All Blacks are not in crisis or anything like that,' he said. 'One player can't make that much difference. They lost two games against a very good South African side.'

The All Blacks, Stephen Donald included, were dominated by the Springboks in 2009, losing all three tests against their historic rivals.

But 10 days after the Durban loss, Carter was back in the All Blacks squad. Said Henry: 'He is a key member of the All Blacks, has recovered well from his injury and has made a great return to rugby so now is the right time to bring him back into the squad.'

With him back in the squad, the debate began to rage as to whether he should start the test from the field or bench. And it was his third outing for Canterbury in a 46–13 win against Waikato that went a long way to convincing Henry it would be the field. He outplayed Donald — his opposite in the Waikato side — steering his team effortlessly around the park while collecting a 19-point haul. Carter would even go on to help his

province lift the Ranfurly Shield with a stellar display in the team's 36–14 win against Wellington. Carter's love affair with Canterbury — questioned by many a year earlier — was now complete.

Ahead of the Sydney test, former skipper Tana Umaga warned the All Blacks not to rely on the returning superstar. 'It's not about saying to Carter and the other new guys, "right, now you're here, let's go". That is one worry because it's not just about these guys coming back. The guys already there have to make sure they make it an easy ride for those returning to the side to get back into the groove. So it puts the onus on the guys that are already there, that is what they should be thinking. Seeing these guys coming back, they should be saying "you ride on the back of us" rather than 14 guys rushing to clamber onto Dan Carter's back. It cannot be like that.'

Umaga need not have worried, as Carter, like it or not, was accustomed to carrying the team on his back, and it was no different in his dramatic reintroduction to test footie. It was his penalty with two minutes remaining that handed the All Blacks a 19–18 win to retain the Bledisloe Cup. Having trailed by nine points at the break, the All Blacks scored the only try of the night and kicked three second-half penalty goals to the Wallabies' two.

Carter made his presence felt in the fourth minute, slotting a penalty goal from 38 metres out. But their advantage was short-lived as the Wallabies hit back with consecutive penalties in the sixth and 10th minutes, off the boot of Australia's first-five-eighth Matt Giteau, to edge in front. Both sides looked to run the ball at every turn, but it was the All Blacks who had the first genuine chance with only a scrambling Giteau denying the visitors in the 25th minute. The Wallabies steadied and had their best attacking opportunity of the half in the shape of an attacking scrum, only to be denied when prop Al Baxter conceded a free kick for collapsing the scrum. Giteau's third penalty against the run of play extended the advantage and, while both sides came agonizingly close to scoring in the

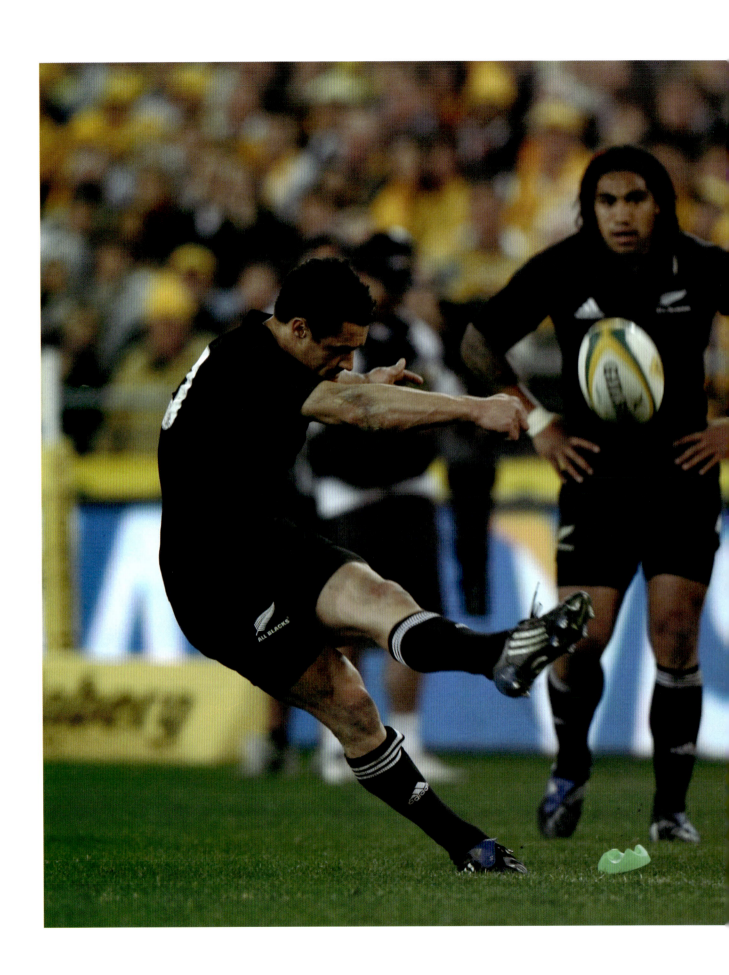

shadows of halftime, the Wallabies had the final say to head to the break with a 12–3 lead.

Carter and Giteau traded penalties at the beginning of the second stanza, before Carter and halfback Jimmy Cowan seemingly scored tries, only to be denied by referee Jonathan Kaplan on both occasions. But the All Blacks stayed on the attack and again trimmed the lead to six with Carter's third penalty, before the Wallabies' defence finally cracked when replacement centre Ma'a Nonu completed a brilliant backline movement for the first five-pointer of the night. Carter's conversion handed the All Blacks their first lead of the night at 16–15, but it was short-lived as Giteau put the hosts back in front with his sixth penalty with 13 minutes on the clock. But Carter had the final say in the 78th minute as the All Blacks repelled a desperate Wallabies raid after the siren to claim a famous victory.

Carter had butchered a dropped goal attempt five minutes from time before pinning the Wallabies inside their 22 with a tactical kick from where the All Blacks won the penalty for Carter to convert. 'I joked with the boys I had to make up for that attempt by slotting that goalkick at the end. [And] with kicks like that you just have to go through your usual routines and you can't worry about what's riding on it and treat it like any other kick,' said Carter, who also talked about the step up to test football from the Air New Zealand Cup. 'It was a huge step up in intensity, physicality and speed and I just really enjoyed being out there. It was tough and very challenging at times and the Wallabies put us under a lot of pressure and got a lot of turnovers in what was a pretty frustrating first half. We got isolated when we got opportunities and they got turnovers so to come back the way we did in the second half . . . was a good comeback.'

Daniel Carter relished his return to the side, and played the role of hero in the thrilling win in Sydney against the Wallabies.

Henry was thrilled with Carter and the win. 'I'm just very proud of the character shown by the players,' he said. 'The win's the result of a lot of mental toughness. We didn't really get the roll of the dice and we kept on coming back and fronting up.' Even Robbie Deans — the Wallabies coach, winless against the All Blacks since the first Bledisloe Cup test of his tenure in 2008 — doffed his hat to Carter. 'Dan Carter showed his class in the last ten minutes converting field position into points. It was there for us, but still not quite there,' Deans said. 'The most obvious difference is experience. They're masters at getting home and we're working hard at acquiring that art. We're making headway but we haven't acquired it yet. I'm pretty confident we will.'

The win meant the Tri-Nations title was on the line when the Boks arrived in New Zealand for a test in Hamilton. For Henry's team to win the competition, they would need a win against the South Africans and another against Australia in Wellington. Certainly the All Blacks were up for the task — driven by the memory of back-to-back losses in South Africa. 'It's about personal pride I suppose,' assistant coach Steve Hansen said. 'They know that we got beaten over there fair and square and you don't like that when you're a competitor and you want to square the ledger.'

Carter, too, noticed a steely resolve from his teammates. 'Most of the team is hurting after that [South African] experience and are looking to bounce back from those tough defeats. There is no better way than to beat the Springboks.' Hansen said it would come down to attitude. 'Attitude is something you've got to build within yourself for the whole week. It's going to hurt, there's no doubt the test match will hurt because they're going to be pretty desperate themselves. You've just got to be prepared to go to the wall.'

The All Blacks don't hold the mortgage on attitude, though, and it was the Boks who would prevail in Wellington 32–29 — a third consecutive win against the All Blacks in 2009. For Carter it was a forgettable night: despite slotting home 19 points, he was guilty of throwing Jean de Villiers the try-winning pass, then

The All Blacks' luck ran out against the Springboks in Hamilton, as the Africans won in New Zealand for the second consecutive year, leaving Daniel Carter, John Afoa, Jimmy Cowan and Ma'a Nonu feeling the pressure.

delayed too long when he could have put Isaac Ross away in the corner. Still, with a bit of razzle dazzle the All Blacks won the last 30 minutes of the game 17–3, and that was enough to convince Carter that an improved brand of rugby was on its way back to the team. 'Hopefully that last 30 minutes, we really grew as a team. We were under the pump a bit and had to really play well. We have to take that and start the next game like that with that confidence and play for a full 80 minutes like that.'

Carter knew an improved performance against the Wallabies in Wellington was as important for the team as it was for the supporters. 'It's just not up to standard. We really want to go into this game and fix the mistakes we've been making in the Tri-Nations and really finish the campaign strong. I think we've got the players in our team to do it and we've shown it in patches. It's a matter of going out and trusting each other for the full 80.'

Typically he, and the team, bounced back with the win against the Aussies — this time by the scoreline of 33–6.

The Tri-Nations hadn't been won. And there were three losses to South Africa to contemplate. But All Blacks rugby looked to be in a better place than it was at the beginning of the domestic test season — thanks to the return to the fold of Carter. But with the All Blacks coaches taking the extraordinary step of switching roles before the end-of-year tour, things were far from perfect as the team contemplated a tough tour.

WITH the World Cup only two years away, the rugby nation was looking for a dramatic improvement to convince them things were on track when the All Blacks assembled for their 2009 Northern Hemisphere tour which would take in — after the one-off test against the Wallabies in Tokyo — games against Wales, Italy, England and France.

There was something of a 'new dawn' vibe to the touring party named by Graham Henry (the new forwards coach), Steve Hansen (the new backs coach) and Wayne Smith (the new defence coach). There were four new caps — first-five-eighth Mike Delany (27), wing Zac Guilford (20), fullback Ben Smith (23) and utility back Tamati Ellison (26) — while lock Isaac Ross, wings Joe Rokocoko and Hosea Gear, and hooker Aled de Malmanche were all left out.

Henry was taking no chances against the Wallabies in the tour opener, despite the Bledisloe Cup being locked away after Carter's heroics in Sydney. He named a full-strength side for a game which was as much about streaks as winning — from the media's point of view anyway. The New Zealanders hadn't lost to Robbie Deans's Wallabies since July 2008, and they knew a win at Tokyo's National Stadium would make it seven consecutive victories. That would equal their second-best trans-Tasman winning sequence, which began in July 1995 and was ended at seven by the Wallabies' 24–16 win at the Melbourne Cricket Ground two years later.

But any talk of the streak was, Carter said, banished from any conversations within the team's confines. 'It's not something that we talk about. Obviously we've been pretty successful against them, but that all unravels if we lose this weekend which we don't want to do. There have been a couple of close encounters . . . Sydney could have gone either way. We've shown some great self-belief in the side and a few times we've played them we've come off a loss and been pretty desperate. When we've lost a couple of games we tend to bounce back pretty well.'

With the dominant record, would the All Blacks lack motivation? With the game being played at the stadium where Peter Snell had won a gold medal at the 1964 Olympics, there was plenty of motivation. And, said Carter — who was closing in on another point-scoring milestone, with his 185 against Australia now just 17 short of Andrew Mehrtens's record of 202 — 'We're playing a team who are always extremely competitive against us, and we really want to get our tour off to a good start and there's only one way to do that, and that's winning.'

Carter certainly did his part, kicking eight from eight for a 22-point haul in the All Blacks' 32–19 stroll. He was then just 15 points short of Mehrtens's career tally of 967 as the Welsh test loomed. 'I've never really been into records but if I do achieve the odd milestone it is quite a cool feeling. I'm sure this will be something after my career that I'll look back on and appreciate a lot more. He [Mehrtens] was a huge influence when I was a teenager, I looked up to him and watched him play for the Crusaders, then had a chance to play alongside him and follow him around and watch the way he plays. I picked up a few tips from him. He was a key person helping me when I first started.'

Carter's tally had been boosted by 25 tries to Mehrtens's seven, and he admitted the running part of his game in Tokyo was the most satisfying. He took the ball to the line strongly, and said it was his intent to give more defences headaches during the five-match tour of Europe. 'It's a real emphasis. I play my best when I'm attacking the line and being a threat, it'll open up space out wide and get us on the go-forward. It's something I'm trying to do but you need that good quality ball and we got it.'

The way Carter had bounced back from his injury to be so dominant six months after his comeback caught the imagination of one of the UK's most respected sports writers, Ian Chadband. 'Dan Carter strips all the emotion out of the debate over who is the best rugby player in the world,' he wrote. 'You can shout for your warriors, beat the drum for your inspirational soldiers and scavengers supreme but ultimately, the quiet, consistent excellence of the game's most commanding field marshal speaks eloquently for itself. Time and again, Carter has offered cool, calculating, occasionally dazzling demonstrations of his pre-eminence as the near-perfect 10, the finest all-round footballer. If we had forgotten this during his absence with a ruptured Achilles, then just a glimpse of the rebuilt Carter dominating in the All Blacks' emphatic Tokyo triumph over Australia should have been enough.

Ahead of the All Blacks' European jaunt, there was the small matter of a Bledisloe Cup test against Australia in Tokyo. Daniel Carter scored 22 points in the 32–19 rout.

'The ring rust from his six-month break had been shed; Dan the main man, who so brilliantly orchestrated four straight New Zealand Tri-Nations triumphs and their British Grand Slam this time last year, was back. Here was game management at its most authoritative. Directing affairs with pinpoint positional kicking, keeping the Wallabies second guessing with his sniping breaks at the line, constantly linking and supporting the attacks effectively while also forcing a key turnover with rock-solid defence. His goal-kicking? Eight from eight. Even after suffering the calf injury which should not stop him demonstrating his renaissance here this next few weeks, he controlled the game effectively on one leg. And just because he is feted as some pretty poster boy, don't think he isn't every bit as crucial to the All Blacks as Richie McCaw. Indeed, the All Blacks' winning percentage when he plays is even fractionally higher, 87.3 per cent, than when McCaw is in the line-up. He'll never surpass [England's] Jonny Wilkinson until he's led New Zealand to a World Cup triumph, his detractors bray, but do not be surprised if Carter's enduring luminous quality puts all arguments clinically to bed come 2011.'

Carter, with a slight calf strain, was in doubt during the build-up to the test in Cardiff, but would end up taking his place in the team, which included six changes from Tokyo. Guilford was given his debut in place of Sitiveni Sivivatu, while Brendon Leonard was selected ahead of Jimmy Cowan at halfback, Wyatt Crockett replaced the suspended Tony Woodcock in the front row, Tom Donnelly made way for Jason Eaton at lock, Jerome Kaino was back at No. 6 in place of Adam Thomson, and Kieran Read was picked at No. 8 ahead of the disappointing Rodney So'oialo.

Carter's 14 points in the 19–12 win against the Welsh was impressive, but he was in the news for a different reason post-game. Carter tackled reserve halfback Martin Roberts around the throat when Wales were building a promising attack in the All Black 22. The officials missed it and Carter avoided sanction. 'They should have had 14 men for the last ten minutes,'

was the sole and no-nonsense post-match input from Welsh defensive coach Shaun Edwards. Warren Gatland — Wales's New Zealand coach — was more forthright. 'It was a head-high tackle. You feel if the guy had made the break in the other 22 it would have been a yellow card and penalty . . .'

The end of the game didn't bring an end to the controversy. After being jeered off the pitch, he was cited for the dangerous tackle by Australian match commissioner Scott Nowland. Roberts also admitted Carter had apologized to him after the tackle. 'Looking at the replay it did look quite high,' Roberts said. 'He did apologize to me. He said "sorry for the tackle"

Daniel Carter was the most hated man in Wales after this high shot on Welsh star Martin Roberts. Carter would be banned for one game after an IRB judiciary meeting.

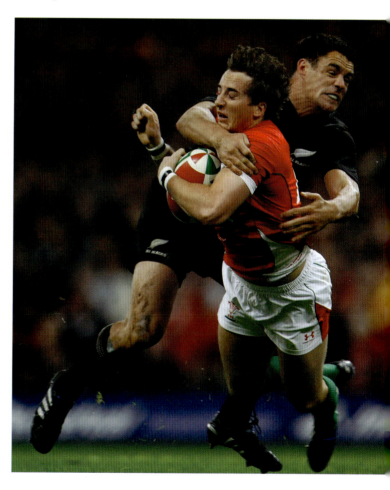

after the game.' The admission was seized upon by the UK press as an admission of guilt rather than what it was intended as: sportsmanship.

For his part, Carter — ahead of the judiciary hearing — told the press that the tackle 'was just one of those things' and that it 'wasn't intentional'. Said Carter: 'It's a tough one but I can't worry too much. I've just got to go there and put my case. I've never been to anything like this before so it's something new for me. I guess I'll worry about it when I'm there.'

Carter was represented by London-based lawyer Owen Eastwood and accompanied by Hansen, who had represented fellow All Blacks Sitiveni Sivivatu (dangerous tackle) and Tony Woodcock (striking) when they received one-match bans in Tokyo. And it would be the same result at the end of the London hearing, meaning Carter would miss the test against Italy in Milan — a game that he was always unlikely to play, given the necessity to have him fit for the tests against England and France that followed in consecutive weekends. Carter and the All Blacks declined to challenge the decision after it was made clear that had it not been for his clean record — he has never been sinbinned as a professional — he would have been given a two-week ban.

All the controversy didn't affect his star power in Italy, though. At an adidas event Carter hit a target, with a ball from 40 metres away, three times in a row, and once with a soccer ball. Then Carter was asked some questions by a local TV star. The conversation went something like this.

Question: Can you present yourself to the Italian public?

Carter: OK, in English? Hi. I'm Dan Carter — unfortunately my Italian is not very good so it will be in English.

Question: OK, in English.

Daniel Carter may not have been the flavour-of-the-month after his performance in Wales, but the Italian fans would take to him a week later.

Carter: Hi. I'm Dan Carter from the All Blacks and we're looking forward to the game against Italy this weekend.

Question: What do you do when you're not playing rugby? Do you like music?

Carter: I love music. I'm learning to DJ at the moment and also love fashion so it's fantastic to be here in Milan for the best shopping in the world.

Question: What is your budget for the week?

Carter: I'll probably use my credit and probably blow that with all the great shops here like Dolce and Gabanna . . .

After confirming Carter used to practise the haka in front of the mirror when he was a kid, there was one last request.

Question: Say ciao in Italian.

Carter: Ciao.

The interview, as basic as it was, turned out to be more entertaining than the rugby served up at the San Siro Stadium as the All Blacks — with Delany in at No. 10 one of 12 changes to the team that beat Wales — stumbled their way to a 20–6 victory.

In truth, it was good when the test was over, because the tour's success would be decided within the next 14 games. The first test would come against the English at Twickenham. And with Carter just one point off equalling Mehrtens's All Blacks points-scoring record, it was a time for reflection. Carter said the ban was a motivating factor for him. 'If anything, that makes me more motivated. I'm fresh. I was happy with the way I played in Wales but I still think I can play better. I want to continue with my running game. I showed little signs of that [in Wales] but a lot goes into that with the forwards getting front-foot ball, then I really want to keep steering them around the paddock; keep working on my vision and attacking where the space is.'

The Twickenham date pitted Carter against Jonny

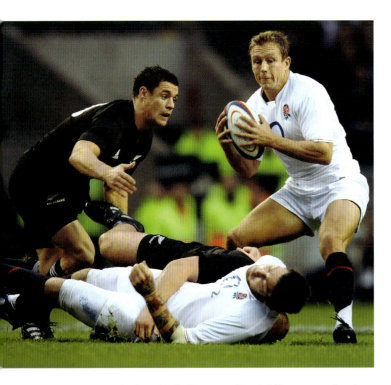

After missing the Italian test, Daniel Carter was back to his best with a 14-point effort against England at Twickenham.

Wilkinson for the first time since the 2005 Lions series. 'He poses a real threat and you just love coming up against guys you admire and respect. That's a great strength of his game, his physicality. He's always going to give 100 per cent and put his body on the line.'

Wilkinson, too, was singing his rival's praises. Said Wilko: 'He's smart, he's switched on and he's obviously a deep enough character to take on things like big injuries and to challenge himself by moving to France. He's got the personality and character and the skills, and without a doubt he's got the faith of his team.'

And that faith was only entrenched even more after another 14-point haul helped the All Blacks to a 19–6 win as they kept their opponents tryless for a seventh consecutive Northern Hemisphere international. Carter's total pushed him past Andrew Mehrtens's test-points scoring record of 967, while his desperate tackle on try-bound England replacement Tom Croft in

the 73rd minute also saved the All Blacks from a tense finish as they defended their line desperately. 'It was tough, but we are happy to get a win at Twickenham,' Carter told Sky Sports. 'It is never easy and there are certainly parts of our game we need to improve on. Defensively we were very sound. But in terms of our attacking ability we have got to hold onto the ball more and build the phases.'

Regarding the record, he said: 'It's a great feeling, I'm very proud. It's something I'll look back on at the end of my career more so and be very happy with it. To overtake a good mate like Mehrts is something I'm pretty happy with. Hopefully there are a few more points to be scored yet.'

Carter had missed his first penalty attempt from in front, and kicked five from seven in all. Going into the test he'd kicked 13 from 13 in Tokyo and Cardiff, before his one-match high-tackle suspension. 'We're used to perfection, aren't we? When he misses a couple of goals it's not perfection for him, so he'll be disappointed in that,' Henry said. 'But he's a big defender and a critical man in the side. You can't expect to have a 10 out of 10 every week, 9.5 is not bad.'

Carter acknowledged his record-breaking feats came with a fair dose of frustration. 'It was pretty frustrating with ball in hand, things weren't gelling as well as we would have liked. Missing a couple of easy kicks is never much fun. But you take the good things with the bad and I was extremely happy with my defensive game, not only myself but the team, we really got off the line well and that's what set us up.'

And Hansen — while happy with the win — knew there was more left in the All Blacks' tank. 'The boys countered well,' he said. 'It comes down to them having faith in their ability, then backing their instincts.

Daniel Carter pushed past Andrew Mehrtens's record All Blacks test-points tally in the game against England. 'It's something I will look back on at the end of my career and be very happy . . .'

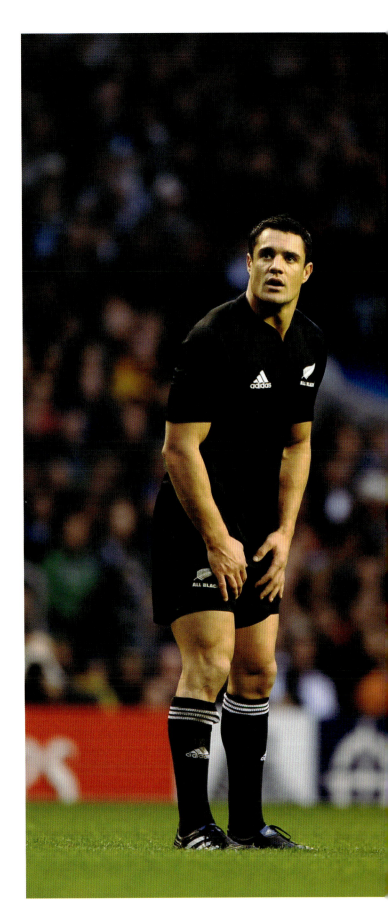

People worked hard to get back and I think we were a bit unlucky not to crack them wide open on a few occasions. On another day we may have. The pleasing thing is we're starting to exhibit the traits that you'd like to see. One day luck will fall our way and we will open someone up pretty big.'

The British press, too, weren't impressed with the All Blacks' performance. British rugby writer Stephen Jones has described the All Blacks as one of the worst New Zealand sides in recent memory. Writing in the *Sunday Times*, Jones said the All Blacks' win was nothing short of a humiliation for England. 'The truth must be grasped. This was the least impressive, least dynamic and least effective New Zealand team I have ever seen play at Twickenham,' Jones wrote. 'The visitors in black fell so dramatically short of their billing that, frankly, they could have been anybody. Aside from some nice touches by Dan Carter and Mils Muliaina, the usual dazzling attack and pace had alarmingly disappeared. If you took Richie McCaw out of their back row, you would have a back five of nothing more than mediocrity at this level, and no team will ever deem themselves without a chance against New Zealand should they be confronted by the fragility of Jimmy Cowan at scrum-half.'

And in the *Guardian*, Paul Hayward lamented: 'The first 20 minutes were a symphony of defiance, as Martin Johnson's mob grasped the reality that the All Blacks come in two forms: the Brazil of the oval ball game, and the panicky, exasperated fumblers of many a World Cup anticlimax. Given licence to play, New Zealand will smash your dreams. Assailed from the first whistle, they will scramble for their patterns and rhythms and resent the interventions of lesser beings. This is a fault line in All Black rugby, but to exploit it England required more than John Bull tenacity.'

The criticism laid the foundations for what would be one of the most impressive performances in All Blacks rugby seven days later in Marseille against France. And Hansen's warning about 'opening someone up' would prove prophetic. The assistant coach was front and centre for setting the tone for the test at a venue where the French had lost only once (to Argentina) in nine outings. The players did have something to hold onto, though: memories of a World Cup win against Italy at the stadium in 2007. 'The one match we had here was against Italy and it was probably our best game of the whole tournament,' Hansen said. 'You can hang onto [the disappointment of the World Cup campaign] or you can decide it's something we've learned from and all moved on from, and we're a better group of people and team because of it.'

Going into the test, the French, like the All Blacks, had good form. They had beaten South Africa in Toulouse a couple of weeks before the All Blacks game, and they could draw on their success in Dunedin to convince themselves they could once again beat the New Zealanders. Henry knew the French would back themselves and selected his strongest side: Mils Muliaina, Cory Jane, Conrad Smith, Ma'a Nonu, Sitiveni Sivivatu, Dan Carter, Jimmy Cowan, Kieran Read, Richie McCaw (captain), Jerome Kaino, Tom Donnelly, Brad Thorn, Neemia Tialata, Andrew Hore and Tony Woodcock. The bench was made up of Corey Flynn, Owen Franks, Anthony Boric, Tanerau Latimer, Andy Ellis, Stephen Donald and Luke McAlister. But for the injured Ali Williams, Richard Kahui and Keven Mealamu, this was the strongest side the All Blacks could have fielded.

And they played like it.

The All Blacks backs cut loose at Stade Velodrome to race in five tries to none and reclaim the Dave Gallaher Trophy in the most emphatic of ways. The 39–12 victory was the most clinical of any All Blacks performance since the 2007 World Cup, and sent a message to the rugby world that the team was to be feared again. Sivivatu, Muliaina, Kaino, Jane and Smith

Daniel Carter and his All Blacks teammates produced the game of Graham Henry's tenure when they beat France 39–12 at Marseille.

scored the All Blacks' tries, while Carter kicked six from seven for a 14-point haul as he guided a hungry backline around before a stunned home crowd of 60,000. After much hand-wringing over the state of test rugby, the All Blacks showed there was still room for an open, running game as they punched away at the fringes and counter-attacked brilliantly, with Muliaina producing another standout performance at the back.

'That's the way you play the game,' McCaw said after the stunning performance, on a night which was a double celebration for the skipper who was named as the IRB's Player of the Year. He felt the turning point of the test was when the All Blacks scrum demolished the French, who had dominated the shoves until that point, and set up a try to Kaino. That made it 22–9 just before halftime, and McCaw could sense the French challenge was waning. 'When you know you've got one more left you can dig pretty deep. The guys were pretty keen, we'd been close in most of the games to putting a performance together. They knew it was going to be tough, but all that together made it pretty easy to get up for the game.'

McCaw became the first person to win the award twice, after scooping it in 2006, as he beat Springboks Francois Steyn and Fourie du Preez, Wallaby Matt Giteau, Ireland pair Brian O'Driscoll and Jamie Heaslip, and England loose forward Tom Croft for the honour. 'I think of all the great players around the world, to be singled out is pretty humbling. But in a team sport it's hard to pick one guy out, and you can't pick up awards like that if you haven't got a team that's pretty special. We've had a challenging year but everyone in the latter half of the year has stood up. I'm proud to be a part of that. It's nice to pick up individual awards, but you've got to always remember that it's your mates outside you that deserve some credit, too.'

Muliaina said McCaw's contribution remained immense. 'He's world-class, probably between him and Dan Carter for best in the world. It's great for them to recognize Richie like that, and the guys are

Two of the best: Daniel Carter (left) and Richie McCaw (above) were hailed after the All Blacks' European exploits in 2009.

just delighted. He's a great leader and a great rugby player and we're stoked for him.'

While McCaw was collecting the silverware, Carter had scribes in all corners of the world singing his praises. Gregor Paul, writing in the *Herald on Sunday* in Auckland said that the common thread in all of the All Blacks' recent best performances was the Cantabrian. 'The All Blacks are a different side when Carter backs himself and is in the mood; when he finds that little bit of extra pace, that explosive acceleration and punishing fend. When he's on, as he was in Marseille and as he was a couple of times [in 2008] and as he most definitely was in the second test against the British Lions in 2005, then the All Blacks are deadly. The All Blacks are untouchable even. When Carter is prepared to back his instincts and really attack the line, he transforms the attacking threat of the All Blacks.

There is no doubt they are a significantly better side when they keep the ball in hand, keep the tempo up and use the width. When the All Blacks play at pace and feed off the holes Carter creates, they are too good for everyone — including South Africa.'

And in the *New Zealand Herald*, Dylan Clever included Carter in the newspaper's Team of the Decade alongside fullback Mils Muliaina, wings Doug Howlett and Joe Rokocoko, centre Tana Umaga, second-five Aaron Mauger, halfback Justin Marshall, No. 8 Rodney So'oialo, flankers Richie McCaw and Jerry Collins, locks Chris Jack and Brad Thorn, hooker Anton Oliver, and props Carl Hayman and Tony Woodcock. Of Carter he wrote: 'Basically [he's] a rugby genius. When Carter is on song, which is most of the time, he makes rugby look ridiculously easy. He can kick for space, he can kick for territory, he can kick goals; he glides through gaps, he can run over fellow fly halves; he passes beautifully; he tackles brilliantly. What more can you ask for? Well, would a World Cup be too much to ask?'

And from Peter Bills — the UK journalist who has studied Carter's career like no other — came this: 'Unless you subscribe to the bizarre theory that it's best to wait until someone has retired or died before offering praise for their talents, let us salute one particular, unique performer from the world of rugby as 2009 comes to its end,' he wrote in *The Independent*. 'Dan Carter is the "Koh-i-Noor" diamond of his time. He glitters as no other jewel can; his quality is simply breathtaking. It has been said that whoever owned the Koh-i-Noor ruled the world. The exact meaning is, "Mountain of Light".

'Well for sure, Carter is a wondrous beacon to those who watch this game. And as for owning the world; well, we'll know whether Carter's country achieves that at the Rugby World Cup in 2011. Rugby, of course, is a team game but let's put it this way: with Carter, New Zealand stands a very decent chance of ending their 24-year wait for a second World Cup triumph. Without him, they have next to no chance.'

'Dan Carter is the "Koh-i-Noor" diamond of his time. He glitters as no other jewel can; his quality is simply breathtaking.'

Bills raved about Carter's performance in Marseille. 'The All Blacks' five tries to nil thrashing of France in Marseille was not entirely due just to Carter. But he lit the touch paper, he was the one who was fundamental to the performance. His decision-making was perfect, his running clever and his chosen angles of attack judicious. He controlled the game throughout with an (apparently) light hand on the tiller. Yet none could doubt his crucial influence. When he struggled into the French hospital on crutches in early February for a critical operation, none knew whether he would ever be quite the same player again. You don't have to be a New Zealander to celebrate his recovery and marvel at the man's restoration to his best.'

'I LOVE this game and I love this life,' Dan Carter says.

'It is the game I love, and that pleasure has never diminished. Your dream as a youngster is to become an All Black. When you do that, you think: "What next?" Now, my dream is being an All Black great. But to do that you have to spend a lot of time in the jersey and play a lot of games. You always have to be the best. That gives me the motivation to work even harder, to keep improving my game, never to be complacent and always to be that little bit better. I always want to have that drive and ambition, because you wouldn't last very long if you just played for the sake of playing. If that were the case, you would do it in a half-hearted way and wouldn't get the enjoyment out of it that I do now. That is the difference between being a great and just playing a couple of matches.'

Dan Carter won't be judged on the 2011 World Cup. If the All Blacks win, he will forever be remembered and hailed in the same breath as players from the 1987 side like Grant Fox, Wayne Shelford and John Kirwan.

If the All Blacks fail to deliver the William Webb Ellis Cup for the sixth consecutive time, he will be cast simply as a 'great'.

That status, already guaranteed.

STATISTICS

- (+) = substitute; (–) = replaced

CANTERBURY

2002	9 games — 35 points
2003	DNP
2004	8 games — 114 points
2005	2 games — 12 points
2006	2 games — 30 points
2007	DNP
2008	DNP
2009	4 games — 76 points

CRUSADERS

2003	13 games — 102 points
2004	14 games — 201 points
2005	12 games — 171 points
2006	15 games — 221 points
2007	6 games — 76 points
2008	11 games — 154 points
2009	DNP

PERPIGNAN

2008–09	5 games — 45 points

ALL BLACKS

2003

21 Jun	v **Wales** at Hamilton 55–3
28 Jun	v **France** at Christchurch 31–23
26 Jul	v **Australia** at Sydney 50–21 (+)
11 Oct	v **Italy** at Melbourne 70–7
17 Oct	v **Canada** at Melbourne 68–6
24 Oct	v **Tonga** at Brisbane 91–7
8 Nov	v **South Africa** at Melbourne 29–9 (+)
20 Nov	v **France** at Sydney 40–13 (+)(–)

2004

12 Jun	v **England** at Dunedin 36–3 (–)
19 Jun	v **England** at Auckland 36–12 (–)
10 Jul	v **Pacific Islanders** at Albany 41–26
17 Jul	v **Australia** at Wellington 16–7
24 Jul	v **South Africa** at Christchurch 23–21 (–)
7 Aug	v **Australia** at Sydney 18–23 (–)
13 Nov	v **Italy** at Rome 59–10
20 Nov	v **Wales** at Cardiff 26–25
27 Nov	v **France** at Paris 45–6

2005

10 Jun	v **Fiji** at Albany 91–0 (–)
25 Jun	v **British & Irish Lions** at Christchurch 21–3
2 Jul	v **British & Irish Lions** at Wellington 48–18
6 Aug	v **South Africa** at Cape Town 16–22
13 Aug	v **Australia** at Sydney 30–13 (–)
5 Nov	v **Wales** at Cardiff 41–3
19 Nov	v **England** at London 23–19

2006

24 Jun	v **Argentina** at Buenos Aires 25–19
8 Jul	v **Australia** at Christchurch 32–12
22 Jul	v **South Africa** at Wellington 35–17
29 Jul	v **Australia** at Brisbane 13–9
19 Aug	v **Australia** at Auckland 34–27
26 Aug	v **South Africa** at Pretoria 45–26
2 Sep	v **South Africa** at Rustenburg 20–21
5 Nov	v **England** at London 41–20

11 Nov	v **France** at Lyon 47–3 (–)
18 Nov	v **France** at Paris 23–11 (–)
25 Nov	v **Wales** at Cardiff 45–10 (–)

2007

2 Jun	v **France** at Auckland 42–11 (–)
16 Jun	v **Canada** at Hamilton 64–13
23 Jun	v **South Africa** at Durban 26–21
30 Jun	v **Australia** at Melbourne 15–20
14 Jul	v **South Africa** at Christchurch 33–6
21 Jul	v **Australia** at Auckland 26–12
8 Sep	v **Italy** at Marseille 76–14 (–)
23 Sep	v **Scotland** at Edinburgh 40–0
6 Oct	v **France** at Cardiff 18–20 (–)

2008

7 Jun	v **Ireland** at Wellington 21–11
14 Jun	v **England** at Auckland 37–20 (–)
21 Jun	v **England** at Christchurch 44–12 (–)
5 Jul	v **South Africa** at Wellington 19–8
12 Jul	v **South Africa** at Dunedin 28–30
26 Jul	v **Australia** at Sydney 19–34
2 Aug	v **Australia** at Auckland 39–10
16 Aug	v **South Africa** at Cape Town 19–0 (–)
3 Sep	v **Samoa** at New Plymouth 101–14 (–)
13 Sep	v **Australia** at Brisbane 28–24
1 Nov	v **Australia** at Hong Kong 19–14
8 Nov	v **Scotland** at Edinburgh 32–6 (+)
15 Nov	v **Ireland** at Dublin 22–3
22 Nov	v **Wales** at Cardiff 29–9
29 Nov	v **England** at London 32–6

2009

22 Aug	v **Australia** at Sydney 19–18
12 Sep	v **South Africa** at Hamilton 29–32
19 Sep	v **Australia** at Wellington 33–6
31 Oct	v **Australia** at Tokyo 32–19 (–)
7 Nov	v **Wales** at Cardiff 19–12
21 Nov	v **England** at London 19–6
28 Nov	v **France** at Marseille 39–12 (–)

POINTS SCORED FOR THE ALL BLACKS

	Tries	Cons	Pens	DGs	Points
v **Wales** at Hamilton, 21 Jun 2003	1	6	1	–	20
v **France** at Christchurch, 28 Jun 2003	–	2	4	–	16
v **Australia** at Sydney, 26 Jul 2003	1	1	–	–	7
v **Italy** at Melbourne, 11 Oct 2003	1	6	–	–	17
v **Canada** at Melbourne, 17 Oct 2003	–	9	–	–	18
v **Tonga** at Brisbane, 24 Oct 2003	1	–	–	–	5
v **France** at Sydney, 20 Nov 2003	–	4	–	–	8
v **England** at Dunedin, 12 Jun 2004	–	3	5	–	21
v **England** at Auckland, 19 Jun 2004	1	4	1	–	16
v **Pacific Islanders** at Albany, 10 Jul 2004	–	4	1	–	11
v **Australia** at Wellington, 17 Jul 2004	–	1	3	–	11
v **South Africa** at Christchurch, 24 Jul 2004	–	–	5	–	15
v **Australia** at Sydney, 7 Aug 2004	–	–	4	–	12
v **Italy** at Rome, 13 Nov 2004	1	7	–	–	19
v **Wales** at Cardiff, 20 Nov 2004	–	1	3	–	11
v **France** at Paris, 27 Nov 2004	1	4	4	–	25
v **Fiji** at Albany, 10 Jun 2005	1	5	–	–	15
v **British & Irish Lions** at Christchurch, 25 Jun 2005	–	1	3	–	11
v **British & Irish Lions** at Wellington, 2 Jul 2005	2	4	5	–	33
v **South Africa** at Cape Town, 6 Aug 2005	–	1	3	–	11
v **Australia** at Sydney, 13 Aug 2005	–	2	3	–	13
v **Wales** at Cardiff, 5 Nov 2005	2	5	2	–	26
v **England** at London, 19 Nov 2005	–	2	3	–	13
v **Argentina** at Buenos Aires, 24 Jun 2006	1	2	2	–	15
v **Australia** at Christchurch, 8 Jul 2006	–	3	2	–	12
v **South Africa** at Wellington, 22 Jul 2006	–	2	7	–	25
v **Australia** at Brisbane, 29 Jul 2006	–	1	1	1	8
v **Australia** at Auckland, 19 Aug 2006	–	2	5	–	19
v **South Africa** at Pretoria, 26 Aug 2006	–	4	4	–	20
v **South Africa** at Rustenburg, 2 Sep 2006	1	2	2	–	15
v **England** at London, 5 Nov 2006	1	3	5	–	26
v **France** at Lyon, 11 Nov 2006	1	3	2	–	17
v **France** at Paris, 18 Nov 2006	–	2	3	–	13
v **Wales** at Cardiff, 25 Nov 2006	–	2	4	–	16
v **France** at Auckland, 2 Jun 2007	–	1	1	–	5
v **Canada** at Hamilton, 16 Jun 2007	3	7	–	–	29
v **South Africa** at Durban, 23 Jun 2007	–	2	3	–	13
v **Australia** at Melbourne, 30 Jun 2007	–	1	1	–	5
v **South Africa** at Christchurch, 14 Jul 2007	1	3	4	–	23

Match					
v **Australia** at Auckland, 21 Jul 2007	–	–	7	–	21
v **Italy** at Marseille, 8 Sep 2007	–	7	1	–	17
v **Scotland** at Edinburgh, 23 Sep 2007	1	2	2	–	15
v **France** at Cardiff, 6 Oct 2007	–	1	2	–	8
v **Ireland** at Wellington, 7 Jun 2008	–	1	3	–	11
v **England** at Auckland, 14 Jun 2008	1	4	3	–	22
v **England** at Christchurch, 21 Jun 2008	1	4	3	–	22
v **South Africa** at Wellington, 5 Jul 2008	–	1	4	–	14
v **South Africa** at Dunedin, 12 Jul 2008	–	1	6	1	23
v **Australia** at Sydney, 26 Jul 2008	–	2	–	–	4
v **Australia** at Auckland, 2 Aug 2008	–	2	5	–	19
v **South Africa** at Cape Town, 16 Aug 2008	1	2	–	–	9
v **Samoa** at New Plymouth, 3 Sep 2008	–	6	–	–	12
v **Australia** at Brisbane, 13 Sep 2008	1	4	–	–	13
v **Australia** at Hong Kong, 1 Nov 2008	–	–	3	–	9
v **Scotland** at Edinburgh, 8 Nov 2008	–	1	–	–	2
v **Ireland** at Dublin, 15 Nov 2008	–	2	1	–	7
v **Wales** at Cardiff, 22 Nov 2008	–	2	5	–	19
v **England** at London, 29 Nov 2008	–	1	5	–	17
v **Australia** at Sydney, 22 Aug 2009	–	1	4	–	14
v **South Africa** at Hamilton, 12 Sep 2009	–	2	5	–	19
v **Australia** at Wellington, 19 Sep 2009	–	3	4	–	18
v **Australia** at Tokyo, 31 Oct 2009	–	2	6	–	22
v **Wales** at Cardiff, 7 Nov 2009	–	1	4	–	14
v **England** at London, 21 Nov 2009	–	1	4	–	14
v **France** at Marseille, 28 Nov 2009	–	4	2	–	14
Totals	**25**	**169**	**175**	**2**	**994**

Cons = conversions

D = drawn

DGs = drop goals

L = lost

P = played

Pens = penalties

W = won

TEST RECORD BY NATION

	P	W	D	L	Tries	Cons	Pens	DGs	Points
Argentina	1	1	–	–	1	2	2	–	15
Australia	16	13	–	3	2	25	48	1	207
British & Irish Lions	2	2	–	–	2	5	8	–	44
Canada	2	2	–	–	3	16	–	–	47
England	8	8	–	–	4	22	29	–	151
Fiji	1	1	–	–	1	5	–	–	15
France	8	7	–	1	2	21	18	–	106
Ireland	2	2	–	–	–	3	4	–	18
Italy	3	3	–	–	2	20	1	–	53
Pacific Islanders	1	1	–	–	–	4	1	–	11
Samoa	1	1	–	–	–	6	–	–	12
Scotland	2	2	–	–	1	3	2	–	17
South Africa	12	8	–	4	3	20	43	1	187
Tonga	1	1	–	–	1	–	–	–	5
Wales	6	6	–	–	3	17	19	–	106
Totals	**66**	**58**	**0**	**8**	**25**	**169**	**175**	**2**	**994**

ABOUT THE AUTHOR

This is John Matheson's 18th book, and 11th rugby title. His previous rugby offerings have included: the bestselling trilogy with former All Black and Sevens star Eric Rush; the No. 1 bestselling biography on All Black great Christian Cullen; tribute books to All Blacks Tana Umaga, Andrew Mehrtens and Richie McCaw, as well as Super coach Robbie Deans; the 2007 biography with living legend Buck Shelford; and *Black Days* — a collection of interviews with the likes of Phil Kearns, Gareth Edwards, Willie John McBride, Francois Pienaar, Serge Blanco and David Campese about the experience of facing the Men in Black.

Outside rugby, his subjects have included biographies with league stars Stacey Jones and Monty Betham, netballer cum cancer-survivor Marg Foster, a tribute to Indy Car superstar Scott Dixon, and books on New Zealand's two successful All Whites World Cup journeys — *All Whites 82* and this year's *All White Fever* — as well as an historical account of the Warriors' first 15 years in the world's toughest league competition.

A six-time recipient at the Qantas Awards, Matheson is now the producer of Martin Devlin's top-rated sports radio show on Radio Live — 'Devlin Does Sport' — and a senior writer for *Truth Weekender*.

He dedicates his part in this book to daughter Ava-Dawn: 'my daytime, my night-time — my world.'

Harper*Sports*
An imprint of HarperCollins*Publishers*

First published in 2010
by HarperCollins*Publishers* (New Zealand) Limited
PO Box 1, Shortland Street, Auckland 1140

HarperCollins*Publishers*
31 View Road, Glenfield, Auckland 0627, New Zealand
25 Ryde Road, Pymble, Sydney, NSW 2073, Australia
A 53, Sector 57, Noida, UP, India
77–85 Fulham Palace Road, London W6 8JB, United Kingdom
2 Bloor Street East, 20th floor, Toronto, Ontario M4W 1A8, Canada
10 East 53rd Street, New York, NY 10022, USA

National Library of New Zealand Cataloguing-in-Publication Data
Matheson, John.
Dan Carter : a tribute to the All Blacks perfect 10 / John Matheson.
ISBN 978-1-86950-869-2
1. Carter, Dan, 1982- 2. Rugby Union football players—
New Zealand—Biography. 3. Rugby Union football—New Zealand
—History.I. Title.
796.333092—dc 22

Cover and internal design by Dexter Fry
Printed in China by Bookbuilders Ltd, Hong Kong

PHOTO CREDITS

TRANZ/Corbis: 2, 4–5, 86, 87, 89, 106, 109, 134–135.
TRANZ/Reuters: cover, 8–9, 10, 13, 14, 16, 18, 19, 21, 22, 23, 24, 25, 26, 27, 28, 29, 30–31, 32–33, 34–35, 36, 37 (top
and bottom), 38–39, 40, 41, 42, 44–45, 46, 49, 50–51, 53, 54–55, 55 (bottom), 57 (top and bottom), 58-59, 60, 61, 62–63,
64–65, 66–67, 68–69, 70–71, 72, 74, 75, 76–77, 78–79, 80, 81, 83, 84, 91, 92, 93, 95, 96, 98–99, 101, 103, 104, 111, 112,
113, 115, 116–117, 118, 120, 121, 122, 124, 124–125, 126–127, 128–129, 130, 132–133, 136–137, 139, 143, back cover.
TRANZ/Eyevine: 6–7.
TRANZ/Zuma: 82.